Management: A Very Short Introduction

Titles in the series include the following:

John Hendry

MANAGEMENT

A Very Short Introduction

OXFORD
UNIVERSITY PRESS

OXFORD
UNIVERSITY PRESS

Great Clarendon Street, Oxford, ox2 6DP,
United Kingdom

Oxford University Press is a department of the University of Oxford.
It furthers the University's objective of excellence in research, scholarship,
and education by publishing worldwide. Oxford is a registered trade mark of
Oxford University Press in the UK and in certain other countries

First Edition published in 2013
Impression: 11

Published in the United States of America by Oxford University Press
198 Madison Avenue, New York, NY 10016, United States of America

British Library Cataloguing in Publication Data
Data available

Library of Congress Control Number: 2013938496

ISBN 978-0-19-965698-1

Printed in Great Britain by
Ashford Colour Press Ltd., Gosport, Hampshire.

Contents

Contents

Preface and acknowledgements

In this book I have sought to provide an introduction to management for three main groups of people: people who may have practised management but have never studied it and are intrigued to know something about the 'subject' of management; people who may have studied it but have never practised it and are interested in how their textbook learning relates to what managers actually do; and people who have neither studied nor practised it but are curious as to what it is all about.

The subject is an enormous one. Hundreds of millions of people around the world are employed as managers of one kind or another. Millions of students take management courses at colleges and universities. And hundreds of thousands of academics teach, research, and publish papers in the subject, in maybe a thousand academic journals. In a short work like this it is impossible to do justice to even a small fraction of that research, but I have tried here to give an outline of how thinking about management has evolved, where it now stands, and how it has impacted and is impacting on management practice.

My own experience of management starts and finishes in practice. I learnt first from my father, Ian, an industrial manager who brought to his job a deep concern for and commitment to the people who worked for him. From him I learnt that people work best when they are happy, appreciated, and can trust in the integrity and fairness of their managers, and that this is especially so when organizations are under pressure and performance is critical. I subsequently found myself managing schools of business and hope that, whatever my limitations, I at least managed to put this insight into practice.

Between these points, after spells in industry, accountancy, the public sector, and a variety of university departments, I studied and taught management as an academic. Among the many people who have influenced me in this period, and whose mark is in some way on this book, two in particular stand out, both of whom I first met as faculty colleagues at the London Business School. One is Charles Handy, whose popular writing on management and organizations has been an inspiration to millions. The other is John Roberts, now at the University of Sydney, who has been a close academic colleague for nearly thirty years and is the most insightful academic researcher I have ever worked with. Both are also brilliant teachers, and both manage, in their different ways, to combine a deep appreciation of the potential lying in every human being with a clear-headed recognition of human frailty. An understanding of what it is to be human and, at the same time, only too human, is at the core of any understanding of management, whether theoretical or practical, and this book is dedicated to Ian, Charles, and John.

Any book like this incurs countless debts, both to other authors (nothing in it is original, except for any mistakes!) and to those who have helped it along the way. I should particularly like to thank David Musson and Andrea Keegan at Oxford University Press for their faith in the project, and Ismael al Amoudi for some stimulating conversations and valuable critiques.

John Hendry
Cambridge, January 2013

List of illustrations

The publisher and the author apologize for any errors or omissions in the above list. If contacted they will be happy to rectify these at the earliest opportunity.

Chapter 1
Management and managing

Introduction

Talking to a friend, John explained that his partner, Mary, was
away for two weeks managing a project overseas, that their son,
Peter, had managed to break a leg playing football, but that he was
just about managing.

When we think of 'management,' the first thing that comes to
mind is an association with work and employment. Management
is what 'managers' do, typically in a business or other
organization, or it is a collective term for these managers, when
contrasted with other employees ('labour' or 'workers') who don't
have the same responsibilities. Managing, in this context, has
strong connotations of being in control, of directing things, of
designing and implementing systems and processes. Outside the
work context, however, we often use the language of managing
ironically, to suggest a lack of control (managing to break a leg), or
as synonymous with coping, or getting by, where control has more
to do with somehow preventing things from falling apart than
with actively directing them.

These colloquial meanings of managing are relatively recent.
The word originates from a Latin term for handling or controlling
a horse, and it was gradually extended from controlling horses

to controlling weapons, boats, people, and, in Britain, affairs more generally. In recent times the meanings of management and its distinction from closely related terms such as administration and direction have slid around across both time and space. In Britain, management has traditionally been associated with business, while the public sector has preferred the term administration. In the USA, business managers (in the British sense) have traditionally been called executives and what they do administration, and management has referred as much to the science of administration as to its practice. In France and Spain, the term management stuck at an earlier stage of its evolution with the management of an athlete or, by extension, a sports team, and other terms have been used to describe management in a business context: *gestion, empresa, direction/direccion, administration/administracion*, etc.

All these terms carry strong connotations of direction and control, but these are particularly marked in the case of 'management,' which is nowadays used globally in a sense that combines the traditional British use, now extended to public sector organizations as well as private sector businesses, with the American overlay of something that can be scientifically researched and studied. So there is a practice of management, which is what hundreds of millions of managers (or administrators or executives or directors) across the world do for a living. And closely associated with this there is an academic subject of management, which is about what managers *should* do, if they are to maximize efficiency or output or profitability, and the fruits of which are currently taught in business schools to millions of students every year.

This book is about both the practice and the subject of management, and much of it will necessarily be concerned with the manager's attempts to exercise direction and control, and with the attempts of management scientists to find ever better ways of doing this. A central theme of the book, however, is that we cannot begin to understand management without also keeping in mind the more colloquial and ironical uses of the term managing. Yes, managers control and direct. But because managers are human, and because the people they manage are also human, things rarely work out quite as intended. So the practice of management is not just about controlling things, but also about coping with things that are out of control—or out of the manager's control—but still have to be dealt with somehow. The study of management, similarly, has to take account of, or find ways to justify not taking account of, the inevitable fallibility and sheer unpredictability of the people who manage and are managed.

This human dimension makes the study of management extraordinarily rich. Like all the social sciences it faces the intriguing challenge of applying rational scientific methods to predict the outcomes of obstinately irrational and unpredictable actors. Unlike many branches of the social sciences, however, management is essentially practical. Its science is developed in order to be used, in the form of organizational technologies, and the consequences of any failure to bridge the gap between assumptions and reality are all too evident. The same human dimension also impacts on the practice of management. Because humans have a propensity to lose or escape control, management as a practice can be immensely frustrating. But for the very same reason it can also be immensely rewarding.

We shall look more closely at the practice of management—at managing, or what managers do—in Chapter 2. First, though, to set the scene, it will help to look a bit more closely at what characterizes us as human beings, and how these characteristics relate to the task of management.

The human condition: reason and its limits

A central concept here is rationality, or the power of reason. Of all the extraordinary abilities that humans possess, the power of reason is probably the most extraordinary. Together with its emotive counterpart, sympathy or human-heartedness, it defines what it means to be human. Its fruits are most strikingly evident in the achievements of science and technology: in computing and communications technologies, biotechnology, medicine, and so on. But it's also a core aspect of everyday life. We may not be great at it, but most of us can argue in a logical, seemingly objective way from premises to conclusions. We can critically assess each other's claims and arrive at sophisticated, evidence-based judgements. And we can formulate and execute complex plans in order to achieve our objectives.

This reasoning ability is central to management. In business schools, in business and management texts, and in many work organizations, management is portrayed as an entirely rational, technical activity. The core of a manager's job, as generally conceived, is to rationally analyse the situations with which she is presented and make rational decisions about how to address them. Businesses and other work organizations are themselves seen as distinctively rational entities devoted to rational ends, most typically the maximization of profit or shareholder value, or the achievement of maximum output for minimum cost.

All this is fine, so long as we don't forget—as people often do forget—that reason has its limits. Some scholars claim that the whole notion of objective reason is a myth. They argue that rationality itself and the sciences built upon it are essentially subjective, the products of a particular society and of the power relations within that society. That is probably going too far. It is true that all scientific theories end up being flawed and inadequate compared with their successors, and the processes by which they change are indeed social and political as much as rational. But their extraordinary predictive success suggests that something pretty objective is going on, in a practical sense if not in a strictly philosophical one. It is perfectly meaningful to talk of scientific rationality, and indeed of objective rationality more generally. The critique of objective reason makes more sense than at first appears, however. The way we think about things, the language we use, and the reasoning we apply are much more subject to social and political forces than we like to think, and we shall explore some of the implications of this for management in Chapter 8. Meanwhile, this critique also alerts us to other, less commonly noted but also less controversial limits on the power of reason.

First, while reason can get us a very long way in our attempts to understand the world, it cannot necessarily get us all the way. Take, for example, the science of quantum mechanics. This is able to predict the behaviour of physical entities far smaller than we can ever observe, to a mind-boggling degree of accuracy, and it has provided the scientific foundation for many of the most powerful technologies of the late 20th and early 21st centuries. But if we try to *understand* it, to imagine what the equations mean in physical terms, we get stuck in hopelessly irresolvable contradictions. At that point, reason runs out on us.

Reason also has a nasty habit of running out on us when things get really important. If we want to ask, for example, whether God exists, or whether there is anything beyond this life, it fails completely. Christian leaders claim that the teachings of Christianity are, to quote a recent pope, 'objective truths'. The leaders of other faiths make similar claims for their own teachings, while militant atheists invoke science to argue, on the contrary, that God does not exist. The fact is, however, that neither the existence nor the non-existence of God can be logically or scientifically proved. Religion attests to the fact that while humans are rational beings we are not *just* rational beings, and it is what we turn to for answers precisely when reason on its own cannot give them.

The most striking feature of the arguments given for the existence or non-existence of God is that every answer is in the end the product of the assumptions, usually unstated, that underlie it. The same is true of arguments in some branches of philosophy, such as ethics, where the only way we can logically prove what is good is by starting from some intuitive or emotional assumption as to what is good. We cannot rationally deduce something from nothing. It is also true of most of the social sciences, including management, which are concerned with behaviours that are far too complex to model accurately, in the way that we model the physical world. And it is true in another sense of much of the reasoning that is conducted in work and everyday life.

By and large, physical entities such as molecules or electrons are well-behaved. They don't forget things, or make mistakes, or change their minds, or fall in love with each other. And since they are well behaved we can both model and predict their behaviour and devise technologies that rely on our predictions. Humans are different. We can sometimes, though not often, predict how they will behave on average or on aggregate. We can very rarely predict, using rational scientific reasoning, how they will behave as individuals.

Rationality and the management challenge

This limit on the power of reason has some fairly obvious implications, not only for the scientific study of management but also for its practice and for the interplay between theory and practice. Let us begin with the sciences of management. Here, as in any science, rationality rules, but in a very compromised form. In order to reach any useful conclusions or predictions, the management sciences have to make some radically simplifying assumptions. Managerial economics, for example, assumes that people are entirely self-interested; that their sole objective is the maximization of financial wealth; that they will do whatever it takes to achieve this, including lying and deceit; and that they will do it with complete competence. Managerial economists don't really believe that all this is true (well, some do, but most don't!), but if they relaxed any one of the assumptions their mathematical models would fall apart and they wouldn't be able to predict anything at all. The assumptions are actually much less extreme than those used in some other branches of economics, and the hope is that they are close enough to reality to make the theories worthwhile.

Managerial psychologists work on completely different but no less controversial assumptions. Some assume particular models of motivation or psychological development while others start from a variety of speculative models of the brain and its operations. Sometimes the insights that result are so striking that we convince ourselves, for a while at least, that the assumptions must be true. What generally happens, though, is that the psychologists' assumptions highlight one distinctive feature of human behaviour by excluding other, equally distinctive but complementary or contrasting features. Each theory is characterized as much by what it obscures as by what it reveals.

Turning to managing, or the practice of management, the rational limitations of humans, whether managers or managed, are only too evident. Contrary to the economists' assumptions, people are not perfectly competent. Indeed they are notoriously incompetent. They are, as we sometimes say, 'only human.' They forget things, get distracted, lose concentration, make mistakes, and get carried away by their emotions. Even the most competent managers have to cope with the human failings (if failings they are) of the people who report to them, as well as with the essential uncertainties of the situations with which they are faced. Managers always have access to more information than they can possibly process, but they never have the information they need to plan with confidence. They face unknown and in many ways quite unknowable futures. And in a business context they face the inherent uncertainties of competition. Reason can help here. As Herbert Simon noted, a rational response to uncertainty, for example, is to limit your research and analysis, make some

7

'reasonable' working assumptions, and get on with things, rather than trying to analyse every conceivable eventuality. But reason alone will never be enough, and especially when dealing with other people the most rational approach won't always be the most effective.

When science and practice come together, in the application of management technologies or techniques, all sorts of things can happen. Sometimes the assumptions underlying the technique are close enough to the reality for it to be effective. One of the recommendations of managerial economics, for example, is that people should generally be incentivized by being paid, wholly or in part, according to their output rather than their input: by piece rates or performance pay. If you're managing fruit pickers, this is quite a good recommendation. They need the money, they are generally competent pickers, and you can measure what they pick, so paying them by the kilo rather than by the hour tends to produce better results.

Applied to other situations, the same technique of performance pay might also work, not because the assumptions reflect reality but because the model itself is more robust than the specific assumptions used to derive it. It turns out, for example, that in many situations the results of the economic 'agency theory' used to model employment contracts are more or less the same as those you would get from the very different (but entirely heterodox) assumption of imperfectly competent but honest and dutiful service. Without direct supervision, it is hard to distinguish laziness from incompetence. Most of us have a bit of both, and the combination is far too complicated to model, but in some cases it doesn't matter too much which we assume to be the case: the same prescriptions work for both.

In other situations, however, the assumptions might not apply at all and the technology might be totally inappropriate. The main area of application of economic agency theory, for example, is to the pay of chief executives and other senior managers. Whether these people are motivated more by the money or by the intrinsic satisfaction of doing a good job is unclear. As career managers in an organizational setting, however, diligence and doing a good job are likely to be quite important to them. Heavily dependent on others in the organization, and in an intensely competitive business environment, their competence is likely to be limited. Not every company can come out on top, after all. We pay chief executives, moreover, to make judgements and exercise discretion, and in doing this we have to assume that they are trustworthy and well motivated. In this context the assumptions do matter, and structuring their pay on the assumption that they are fully competent self-seekers, which is what most large companies now do, will almost inevitably lead to perverse and quite unintended effects.

One of these unintended effects is that when we apply theories with strong assumptions to practice, the assumptions can easily become self-fulfilling. When social scientists assume that people are narrowly self-interested, for example, when teachers convey that assumption to students, and when practitioners implement techniques based upon it, the chances are that people will become narrowly self-interested even if they weren't to start off with. This is most clearly seen in the world of finance, where people now quite consciously behave in the way that finance theory (closely linked to managerial economics) assumes that they behave. This makes for a better match between theory and practice but, as the recent financial crisis has shown, with pretty dire consequences for the rest of us.

Management has not yet reached that stage. Though the science of management is becoming more and more dominated by economics, it also draws heavily on psychology and sociology, and so finds room for a wide range of often conflicting assumptions. This brings its own practical problems, however. Conceived from the start as an aid to practice, the science of management is

9

unremittingly functional. In drawing on more fundamental research in the social sciences it is interested only in what might be useful, and when it borrows ideas and concepts it does so with scant regard for either their underlying assumptions or their scientific validity. The result is a body of work that is often self-contradictory and quite deeply confused, and that tends, when applied to practice, to have correspondingly contradictory and confused results. As we shall see, the history of management, much like the everyday practice of managing, is as much a story of unintended consequences as of intended ones. Before recounting that history, though, let's stop a moment and ask a very obvious but rarely answered question: what exactly do managers do?

Chapter 2
The work of the manager

Of the tens of thousands of books and articles devoted to research in management, remarkably few address what managers do, and their research base is notably narrow. The most influential study, carried out by Canadian academic Henry Mintzberg around 1970, was based on observations of just five senior managers for a week each. Investigating how well Mintzberg's conclusions had stood the test of time thirty years later, Stefan Tengblad studied just four chief executives. For his most recent study, the basis of a book published in 2009, Mintzberg studied twenty-nine managers at different levels of seniority, but spent just one day with each of them. Fortunately, the results of these and the other major studies, about fifteen in all, are all fairly consistent. Different writers interpret their observations in different ways, and there are clearly some variations in the nature of managerial work, both across time and national cultures and with the size and culture of the organization and the seniority of the position. The general pattern, though, seems fairly uniform.

We can look at managerial work in three ways. We can ask what managers do in a functional sense. We can ask about how they do it, or the practice of management. And we can ask about the qualities of this practice. To take a slightly simpler example, if we wanted to describe the work of police officers we might discuss the functions of preventing crime and catching criminals; the practices of patrolling, filling in report forms, breaking up disturbances, making arrests, and so on; and the qualities of commitment, service, and the balance between tedium and excitement. Of course, police work is much more complicated than this brief sketch suggests, and management work (including the management of police work) is much more complex still. The three dimensions are also overlapping and mutually dependent. It is hard to describe the functions without detailing the practices, or to make sense of the practices without invoking the functions. The three dimensions do, however, give us a useful starting point for structuring our discussion.

In this chapter we shall explore managerial work through three functional dimensions abstracted from the various research studies: routine administration, troubleshooting, and leadership. We shall explore each one using a categorization of practice taken from Mintzberg's most recent work, in which he divides managing into the managing that is done in the manager's own head (i.e. thinking), managing through information, managing with people, and managing through direct action. A secondary categorization divides these practices of managing into managing within the unit for which the manager is responsible, managing across to the other parts of the organization, and managing across the organization's boundaries, in relation to customers, suppliers, and other stakeholders. We shall conclude with a short discussion of the quality of managerial work. Figure 1 sets out the framework for the chapter.

Management as routine administration

The defining characteristic of management is responsibility for an organization or organizational unit and for the work of its members. The unit might be anything from a small retail outlet with one or two shop assistants to a large corporation with tens or even hundreds of thousands of employees, but most managers are directly responsible for managing the organization of a

1. Dimensions of managerial work

'manageable' number of people—typically between two and twenty—and of the various processes in which they are engaged. So we have sales managers and production managers and marketing managers and IT managers etc., organizing the work of specialists. Then, at the level of the business unit or agency or regional subsidiary, we have general managers, whose job is to organize and coordinate the work of different specialist groups.

Organizations work by organizing work, but this doesn't happen by itself, and much of the work of managers is concerned with maintaining the organization. At the informational level this entails monitoring what is going on both inside and outside the unit and disseminating information to wherever it is needed. Some of this information comes in the form of reports from below or instructions from above. Some of it comes less formally through conversations and meetings. Managers glean information from the outside world and exchange information with the managers of other units. A good manager is, as Mintzberg puts it, the nerve centre of the unit, more informed than anyone else but also filtering information (processing emails alone can be a very time-consuming task) and acting both as spokesperson *for* the unit, representing it to the outside world, and as spokesperson *to* the unit, representing the outside world to it.

Also at the informational level, managers typically take responsibility for maintaining, adapting, and sometimes designing the structures and systems through which their units operate. Mintzberg describes this in terms of a control function and it is probably the aspect of managing that comes closest to the popular control-oriented conception of what managers do. Managers allocate resources, set objectives, delegate tasks, and authorize actions. From the viewpoint of the people being managed, this looks like the exercise of authority. From the perspective of the manager, much of it is simply routine, and in some respects the most tedious part of the job: making operating decisions, setting budgets, writing job descriptions, signing things off. Occasionally there is a chance to build a new team, set up a new project, or design things afresh, and then things get more interesting, but the more successful the design, the longer it lasts, so in effective organizations the routine will often dominate.

Turning to the interpersonal level, most of the information-processing activities described above also entail managing with people. To maintain their information flows, managers have to be effective networkers, both inside the organization and, in many cases, beyond it. Even in today's world of advanced information systems there is no substitute for personal contact. The better your contacts, the more likely you are to get the information you need. The better you know the person with whom you're exchanging information, the more effective that information exchange is likely to be, and the smaller will be the risk of misunderstanding. The better you know people, too, the more effectively you will be able to coordinate your activities with theirs.

The spokesperson roles also have a strong interpersonal dimension. Representing the unit often has a social and sometimes a public dimension. It involves advocacy, persuasion, promotion, and helping people who might help you. Representing to the unit requires similar skills, and people have not only to be told things but also convinced of them—of a company strategy, for example, or a new human resources policy. Many workers are inherently sceptical of decisions taken elsewhere. Doctors and professors, for example, distrust hospital and university administrators. Divisional outposts and subsidiaries distrust their headquarters. Workers generally distrust 'management'. If the organization as a whole is to work coherently and effectively, managers have to overcome this scepticism in their units and provide a personal bridge between policy and administration. At the same time, they also have to protect their units, and themselves, from unhelpful outside interference: from interfering bosses, from fickle customers, or from pushy salespeople. An important part of managing a unit is managing outside disturbances so that the people in the unit can get on with their jobs.

Finally, the task of maintaining and operating systems is often as much about people as information. You can only allocate duties or set objectives if you know your staff individually and understand something of their own interpersonal relationships. Meetings have to be effectively managed. In more formal organizations, committees have to be effectively chaired. It is the manager's job to ensure that the right voices are heard, and not just the loudest or most persistent. Staff hiring and promotion, review and appraisal are also critical tasks, not only in themselves but as symbolic indicators of a manager's fairness and good judgement, perceptions of which are probably more important than anything in gaining the support and goodwill of staff.

It goes without saying that all of these activities also require managers to spend time thinking, but the old-fashioned idea of a manager as someone who spends time sitting at his desk thinking is a long way from reality. Managers do spend a lot of time thinking about their routine administration, but they do so on the move, en route from one meeting to another, driving to and from work. As for acting directly, carrying out routine tasks alongside the people they manage, many managers do find time for this, but if they do a lot of it, it is probably because they are trying to escape from the proper tasks of management. Successful managers often try to schedule some activity, taking part in project teams or keeping their hand in with their unit's specialist function, mainly to maintain their information flows and personal relationships. But they often find that it gets crowded out of their schedules.

Routine administration is in many respects the least interesting part of managing, but it is also the most time consuming. It is critically important to the smooth running of an organization and many managers seem to enjoy it. It is relatively stress free and can be a welcome distraction from more stressful and demanding tasks. And it brings the little rewards, in a regular fashion, of a job satisfactorily completed as well as of a salary well earned. There is great satisfaction, in particular, in being responsible for a happy and effective team, and especially in seeing that good work and good employees are recognized and rewarded.

Management as troubleshooting

While routine administration may be the most time-consuming dimension of managing, the most preoccupying is troubleshooting, or responding to what the British prime minister Harold Macmillan famously termed 'events'.

Unplanned, unexpected, and often unwanted events happen. Things go wrong. Machines break down. Supplies get delayed.

Workers strike. Competitors steal a march. Customers get upset, with or without good reason. Projects go over budget. Deadlines get missed. Tasks get forgotten, or fall through the cracks. People get ill or have accidents at critical moments. People make mistakes. People get convinced that other people have made mistakes. Colleagues fall out. Rumours spread. The best-laid plans go awry and things don't work out as intended.

In one sense, troubleshooting is itself routine. Given the uncertainties of the social world and the fallibilities of human beings it is inevitable that things will sometimes go wrong. Sometimes problems arise from the manager's own limitations or mistakes (all managers make mistakes, though they may not admit it). Sometimes they arise from mistakes by people for whom the manager is responsible. Sometimes the fault lies outside the unit, and sometimes no one is at fault at all, but the unit still has to respond in some way. Whatever the origins of the problem, the responsibility for troubleshooting generally lies with a manager or group of managers, and it is managers who have the formal authority, the information (as the nerve centres of their units), and the interpersonal resources and relationships needed to take effective action.

Depending on the nature of the problem, managing as troubleshooting may involve any combination of the different levels in Mintzberg's model. It certainly requires thinking, and clear thinking at that—all the harder but all the more necessary in an atmosphere of crisis. It is also when troubleshooting that managers are most likely to get involved in direct action, doing a job themselves that would normally be delegated. Sometimes it is a question of covering for absent or emotionally incapacitated staff: a case of all hands to deck. Sometimes a problem needs the extra knowledge, contacts, or experience that the manager can bring to bear: dealing with an awkward customer, for example, calling in favours to secure a delivery, or finding a technical fix.

When a problem arises from a mistake or mistakes, the interpersonal side of managing becomes crucial. There is very little discussion in the literature of how managers deal with mistakes. It is almost as if the very idea that mistakes can happen runs so counter to the dominant image of management as a technical, rational utopia that it simply can't be accommodated. We all know, however, that mistakes do happen, and how managers respond to the mistakes of their staff can be critical to their success or failure. Is a mistake just an accidental one-off, in which case you might forget it and move on? Is it a sign that the person isn't really up to the job, in which case you will need to work out whether this can be remedied by training and development or whether you need to be looking at competency procedures? Is there an element of wilful neglect, calling for the commencement of disciplinary procedures? Or are there other things going on in the person's life—work relationships, family problems, illness, or depression—that suggest a need for support and counselling? How will the person respond to different reactions on your part? How firm should you be, and how sympathetic?

Different managers have different styles, but all good managers need to measure their responses, balancing particular cases and individual personalities against a general requirement for fairness and consistency. They also need, at a basic level, to respond. Because dealing with people's mistakes can be difficult and stressful, it is very tempting to put it off, to sweep things under the carpet and hope they'll go away. It is a common feature of organizational life that, when the time comes for disciplinary action or action on the grounds of incompetence, it transpires that the person concerned has posed problems of the same kind for years, but nobody has taken the steps of raising the issue, going through the formal procedures, and establishing a paper trail of warnings. So everything has to start from scratch and what should be a final offence becomes a first one. Since the same manager is rarely in place long enough to see these kinds of procedures through, this becomes a collective task, but if it is not done the organization suffers and the other workers in the unit suffer especially. So a critical part of managing is managing to manage, and not just to cope.

How managers deal with their own mistakes is also important. Some managers simply won't admit to any mistakes, of course, and blame anything that goes wrong on someone else. But while this sometimes advances their careers in the short term it doesn't make for effective management. Managers who wallow in their mistakes, however, are no use either. The basic recipe here is simple: minimize the damage (and make sure that the innocent are exonerated), maximize the learning, and act in the best interests of the organization. Putting it into practice, though, can be quite demanding: we shall pick up this theme later, in Chapter 9.

Managers also have to respond carefully to mistakes outside the unit, and tempting as it may be to grasp the opportunity of blaming others, this isn't always the most productive way forward. Here the manager's networks, relationships, and political skills come into play. The task is to solve the problem and move forward, and, as in politics generally, this often requires careful compromises and diplomatic reticence as well as measured assertiveness.

Management as leadership

The ability to cut through a mess of mistakes and mutual recriminations and get everyone moving together again is one we tend to associate with leadership as much as management, and the relationship between these two has long been a matter for debate. Some of the most influential writers on leadership have sought to distinguish it sharply from management. Warren Bennis, for example, has asserted that 'Leaders are people who do the right thing; managers are people who do things right.' Leaders, on this conception, set the strategy and direction of an organization. Managers implement that strategy. Bennis also criticizes leaders, however, for getting sucked into routine management themselves, while other prominent writers, such as Harvard Business School Professors John Kotter and Abraham Zaleznik, have criticized *managers* for getting sucked into routine management. And many of the classic works on management have the word 'leadership' somewhere in the title. On this view, leadership has always been part of management and essential, especially, for the management of change; but it has often been neglected, both in practice and in management development. It can hardly be said to be neglected in management development any more: some business schools seem to do nothing else but leadership development. Fitting it into management practice, however, can still be a challenge.

The history of the relationship between leadership and management is tied up with the history of organizational structures. Fifty years ago most large organizations, whether in the private or the public sector, were rigid hierarchical bureaucracies. In these organizations, direction setting was confined to the top management levels, and the knowledge and understanding needed to compete effectively in business, or to provide effective public services, had been gradually built in over long periods of time to the systems and processes of the organization. These organizations were engineered for stability and their management was naturally dominated by routine administration.

Over the last forty years or so, global competition and massively advanced information technologies have made these large business bureaucracies increasingly vulnerable to faster and more agile competitors. Businesses nowadays have to be engineered for change as much as for stability, and one consequence of this has been a loosening of their bureaucratic structures. All firms retain an element of hierarchy, and strategy setting and overall direction remain largely the preserve of the chief executive and top management team, at least in a formal sense. But within the organization a skeletal hierarchy is now overlaid with flexible networks and self-organizing project teams rather than with the traditional bureaucratic offices. At the same time, the psychological contract between firm and employee has moved away from one based on long-term rewards for dutiful service towards one based on short-term performance incentives. Meanwhile, public sector organizations, driven by demands for efficiency gains, have also moved increasingly towards the business model.

To see how these changes have impacted on the leadership dimension of management, consider John Kotter's summary of the three processes involved in effective leadership:

1. Establishing direction—developing a vision of the future, often the distant future, along with strategies for producing the changes needed to achieve that vision.
2. Aligning people—communicating the direction to those whose cooperation may be needed so as to create coalitions that understand the vision and are committed to its achievement.
3. Motivating and inspiring—keeping people moving in the right direction despite major political, bureaucratic, and resource barriers to change by appealing to very basic, but often untapped, human needs, values, and emotion.

In times gone by, an organizational unit would have its direction set for it. That might still be the case, but in contemporary organizations it may just be the outputs that are imposed, through performance targets. It is then for the manager to set a direction of the unit in order to achieve those targets. In traditional mature bureaucracies a lot of the work of aligning people was done by the formal structures—protocols, manuals, job descriptions, and so on—and by a deeply ingrained organizational culture. In more flexible organizations, where jobs are not tightly defined and people move rapidly between teams, the managers have a lot more work to do. This is as much the case, moreover, in periods of stability as in periods of change. The problem that faced Kotter back in the 1980s was not how people within an organization could be aligned—bureaucracies did that very well—but how people could be realigned to a *new* direction against the deeply conservative forces of the organization. His emphasis on motivating and inspiring was focused on the need to overcome resistance to change. The problem facing managers today is how people can be aligned at all, in the context of rapid organizational changes and terms of employment that play to their individual self-interest. Even holding a team together for long enough to complete a job can be difficult, as people plot their advance through the organization by skipping from team to team, trying to be in the right place at the right time to capture the next opportunity of advancement. Motivating and inspiring people are thus more important than ever, but also much more difficult.

Setting directions, communicating those directions, building coalitions, motivating and inspiring people are all as much part of management as they are of leadership, and in a relatively modest way they are all part of management as routine administration. There is a difference, though, albeit hard to pin down, between motivating and maintaining an effective team or unit, guiding them through a crisis brought on by 'events,' and motivating them, when required, to perform beyond themselves, to break out of their institutionalized comfort zones, or to commit to changes of which they may not naturally be convinced. Although the qualities of leadership are now often needed simply to hold things together and pull people towards a common goal rather than their own individual goals, they are still needed most at times of change, when organizations are being formed or reformed.

Routines, habits, and organizational cultures are part of the way we respond to complexity and uncertainty. Unable to work out what to do afresh each day, we find patterns that work and stick to them. Because these patterns are based on past successes, and because they are essentially techniques for survival, they are immensely hard to shift. Old habits die hard, even more at the institutional than at the personal level. But the world changes, and to keep being successful we have to change with it. The key role of the manager as leader is to initiate and manage such changes, generating the energy levels to lift people out of their established steady states, using the change to enable people's development, and building new habits and a new culture to replace the old.

The quality of managerial work

It should be apparent by now that the work of the manager looks a lot more like the work of someone 'managing' in everyday life—as John was in our opening example—than like the traditional image of a manager in control. As we noted above, the challenge is to get beyond coping, to manage to manage. An effective manager is in control, albeit not completely and often not overtly. But the way in which she is in control and the situations she is in control of look remarkably like a caricature of a harassed parent, with children crying, dogs barking, the telephone ringing, a delivery arriving, guests due, and a fuse blowing, all at the same time.

The quality of managerial work comes across most forcefully from studies of new managers, who soon find out that the job is not at all what they expected; but it is also reflected in the basic data of how managers spend their time. Most studies agree that managers spend the majority of their time, typically around two-thirds, in meetings. The rest is spent mainly on the telephone, travelling between meetings or, nowadays, sending and responding to emails. Little time is spent working at the desk, and reports are more likely to be written or read at home than in the office. The work is highly variable and highly fragmented, comprising anything up to thirty or forty distinct activities in a single day and with critical and mundane tasks interwoven in no apparent order. Managers need to be able to switch moods and modes with alarming frequency.

Managerial work is also very flexible. With so many demands on a manager's time, it is often tightly scheduled, but the schedules change frequently in response to new demands. It has also become immensely time consuming. The managers observed by Mintzberg forty years ago worked immensely hard at an unrelenting pace, but they worked on average a forty-five-hour week. The managers observed by Tengblad more recently worked at the same unrelenting pace but for a seventy-two-hour week, and my own studies suggest that at senior levels this is now the norm. Indeed, the most senior managers typically put in as many hours as they possibly can without consciously becoming dysfunctional. Other recent studies suggest that even middle managers routinely put in fifty- to sixty-hour weeks.

The unrelenting nature of managerial work follows from its being both undefined and unbounded. This comes across especially from the studies of new managers such as those by Linda Hill and Tony Watson and Pauline Harris. Coming from jobs that were both well defined (typically some specialized trade or profession, or a specific set of tasks and duties) and bounded (you finished one task and moved on to the next), those new managers found first that there was nothing to tell them what they should do, and subsequently that there was nothing to tell them what they should not do. The single most striking feature of a manager's work is that it is never done. There is always far more to do than can possibly be done.

This is especially the case in today's more flexible organizations. The general dismantling of bureaucratic offices has taken away the boundaries of a manager's responsibilities. And even the firms that have not moved over to flexible structures have delayered their managerial hierarchies, putting greater loads on their middle managers while at the same time limiting their prospects for career advancement. All this work inevitably impacts on people's home lives and general well-being, and many managers today find their work both stressful and exhausting. But many others—often, the ones lucky enough to have good managers above them—find it exhilarating and rewarding. Again, it's remarkably like being a parent or, for the many managers who are also parents, like having another household and family to cope with alongside your own. We shall come back in Chapter 10 to some of the moral aspects of these demands, but next we shall look at the evolution of management thinking and practice, at the management theories that have been developed, the techniques that have been built upon them, and the ways in which these have impacted on management practice.

Chapter 3
Management and authority

Management, authority, and coercion

The oldest and simplest approach to management is to tell people what to do and make sure they do it, if necessary by using violence or the threat of violence. This basic approach is still the norm in much of the developing world and in most emerging economies. It is still commonplace, subject to various legal constraints, in small owner-managed businesses everywhere. The boss gives instructions and the employees do what they're told, or suffer whatever consequences the boss decrees if they don't.

The earliest roots of management lie in the management of two kinds of organization, both hierarchical in form. One is the extended family, household, or estate, where the people to be managed might include servants or slaves, agricultural workers, and a limited range of specialist trades (cooks, farriers, and so on). The other is the army or, on a smaller scale, the merchant ship.

Both kinds of organization have traditionally relied on a combination of authority and coercion, with the 'manager' being authorized (by society or his peer group) not only to give instructions but also to inflict physical punishment in pursuit of their execution. Well into the 20th century, even in the most 'civilized' societies, soldiers or sailors who disobeyed orders were likely to be flogged or, in extreme cases, executed. In the First World War, both disobeying orders and desertion were capital offences in the armies of both sides, and they remain so in some armies today. On board ship, once on the high seas, the opportunities for escape were small and the threat of violence correspondingly felt.

In the household or estate, authority was traditionally exercised through systems of slavery and bonded labour, with the fear of physical punishment again to the fore. Even when workers were notionally free, they were often severely constrained. Remuneration, for example, would be provided predominantly in kind, through the provision of food and accommodation, meaning that it was almost impossible to leave one job with having another to go to, and almost impossible to get a job without a good reference from the one you were leaving, a classic catch-22 situation. As in the military context, physical punishment was also the norm, with free labourers as well as slaves being subject to beatings if they didn't follow orders, and often if they did.

In the developed world, slavery is nowadays outlawed—though it still exists in a hidden underworld of trafficked prostitutes and domestic servants. In the form of bonded labour, however, it is still very much present in the developing world. Kevin Bales has estimated that in 2000 there were around 27 million people working under conditions of slavery across the world, in countries such as India, Pakistan, Bangladesh, Thailand, and Brazil.

In Thailand and many other countries, young teenage girls are sold to brokers by their parents for the price of a television set. The contract stipulates that the brokers' outlays are recouped from the girls' incomes. But deposited in brothels, raped, and brutalized, the girls never earn enough to repay the debt. With the police bought out by the brothel keepers, escape is impossible, violence is endemic, and the girls work until they are literally used up.

In Brazil, young men are attracted by the promise of well-paid jobs. Driven out to the forests, to vast charcoal camps, they are only then told that they owe a debt to the people who drove them there. With no money, massive 'debt,' and their identity cards confiscated, escape is again impossible and the regime is, again, one of violent coercion.

In the brick fields of Pakistan, whole families are employed in digging clay and making bricks, with the debt incurred when they were first taken on sometimes passed from generation to generation. In India, millions of agricultural workers still live and work under a feudal arrangement in which generation upon generation has been permanently indebted to landowning employers, who pay them no wages as such, just a subsistence living.

Management through coercion is not restricted to bonded labour and the military. If tens of millions work as slaves, hundreds of millions work under oppressive and physically threatening regimes. Despite the spread of human rights and employee protection legislation, many of the world's factories are run with an iron rod. Trapped by economic necessity and the absence of any better alternatives, often living in company-owned dormitories in rapidly expanding cities far from their family roots, many factory employees routinely suffer abuse and intimidation at the hands of their managers. In many smaller organizations, managers act coercively without even thinking about it. They give instructions, and when the instructions are not implemented to their satisfaction they just shout and get angry, and give the instructions again, with threats. Like the bad workman blaming his tools, when anything goes wrong they blame their employees—who are indeed seen as tools. It never occurs to them to question themselves.

Legitimate authority

The exercise of authority doesn't have to be coercive, and even when it is it can take a variety of forms. In the early 20th century the founder of modern sociology, Max Weber, identified and distinguished between three forms of 'legitimate authority,' or three ways in which authority that might be socially grounded and legitimated within a social group.

The first type of authority in Weber's scheme is *traditional authority*, resting on a belief in the sanctity of long-standing traditions and, in particular, on the legitimacy of the social status of those exercising the authority. This would most obviously include the authority of a king over his subjects, a hereditary landowner over his estate, or a father over his family.

The second type is *charismatic authority*, resting on admiration of the qualities of a particular individual and a consequent devotion to that individual, and obedience to the rules or norms proclaimed by him. Examples here include the authority exerted by inspirational preachers or leaders of religious sects, by the leaders of political rebellions, by charismatic generals in the field, or by charismatic entrepreneurs. Although, as Weber noted, charismatic authority can sometimes be transmitted to a chosen successor, it is distinctively personal.

The third type is *rational* or *legal authority*, resting on acceptance of the legal basis of rules and of the rights of duly appointed people to enforce them. This is the authority exercised by officers of state and other public officials, from police officers making arrests to librarians imposing silence. It is the basis of authority in the armed forces and of the authority of managers in a rationally designed organization, the command structure of which is accepted by its members. In a management context it is, especially, the basis of bureaucracy.

Weber stressed that these were analytical 'ideal types' and that any real-world situation was likely to entail combinations of the different types, as well as combinations of consensually and coercively exercised authority. A simple example in illustration would be that of a military officer, drawn from the upper classes of society. Such a person might exercise rational authority, as holder of a particular rank or office; traditional authority, in the eyes of troops drawn from the lower classes; and charismatic authority, on the basis of his own personality. Another officer, lacking charismatic or traditional authority, might rely mainly on the rational authority associated with his office but back that up with the threat or exercise of violence. Unable to draw on the love or respect of his troops, but only their rational acquiescence, he might resort to fear.

An insightful example of how legitimate authority can embrace coercion is given by the writer Sebastian Faulks in his novel *Birdsong*. Set before and during the First World War, this points to parallels between the violence with which one of the characters routinely treats his wife; the violent subjugation by the same character of the workers at his factory; and the violence imposed on conscript soldiers in the trenches, sent by their senior officers 'over the top' to their almost certain deaths, to no obvious end, under threat of execution if they resisted, and with chaplains in attendance. In each case the violence portrayed here was not a counter or alternative to legitimate authority, but a socially legitimized part of that authority. The traditional authority of a husband over his wife included the authority to beat her. The traditional-cum-rational authority of the factory owner included the authority to forcibly subjugate the workers. The rational authority of the officer combines with the traditional authority of the priest to justify sending people to their needless deaths. In many societies today such violence is no longer seen as legitimate. It constitutes an abuse, not an exercise, of legitimate authority. In many other societies, however, little seems to have changed.

The first industrial managers, managing the factories of the industrial revolution in the early 19th century, were either members of the owner's family or, below them, overseers promoted from the workforce for their loyalty and ability to promote discipline. In this arrangement, which is still characteristic of many developing economies, all three kinds of authority are mixed up, with coercion typically filling in for the combined limitations of tradition, charisma, and formal structure.

The administration of authority

This tendency for the different types of authority to operate in conjunction is particularly significant in the case of rational authority, which seems to emerge historically in combination with the simpler forms of traditional and charismatic authority and as a response to their limitations. The rational authority associated with the rank of a military officer, for example, is not just the result of a rational consensus but is rather derived from the traditional authority of king or state.

Both of the simpler forms of authority face limitations of scale and distance, as the holder of authority cannot be everywhere at once and has to act through others, in absentia. This requires delegation, but a simple hierarchy of delegated authority can only get you so far. Exercising authority on a large scale also requires mechanisms for monitoring to check that tasks are properly carried out and for ensuring consistency and conformity. It requires basic technologies of administration and accounting.

These challenges go way back. Consider, for example, the task in classical times of administering the army of ancient Rome and the collection of taxes across an empire stretching from Scotland in the north to Morocco in the west and Iraq in the south-east. In the 16th and 17th centuries the great British and Dutch East India companies, privately owned but state-sponsored corporations, conducted business and administered trading colonies over still greater distances. To operate effectively, these organizations developed increasingly sophisticated systems of accounting and audit and a division of managerial as well as manual labour, leading to particular offices each with its own function and rule book. In the 19th century the administration of vast overseas empires and domestic public services led to further developments in accounting and the collection and use of statistical data. At the same time, the development of large geographically dispersed manufacturing companies on the back of new technologies of railroad, telegraph, and mass production created similar challenges and also created a cadre of specialist engineer-managers with a predilection for rationally engineered solutions.

Bureaucracy

So closely is the theory of bureaucracy associated with Max Weber that many people seem to think he invented bureaucracy, and that the bureaucratic organizations of the 20th century were built to his template. That is certainly not the case. Few managers can ever have gone to Weber for practical guidance, and by the time his classic study, *Wirtschaft und Gesellschaft*, was published, posthumously, in 1922, bureaucracy was very much the established norm for large organizations in both public and private sectors. Weber's analysis is still worth attention, though, for its clarity and insight to the core features of bureaucratic management. According to Weber:

- The basic building block of bureaucracy is the *bureau* or *office*, which is at the same time a (typically managerial) job, a department, and a physical place. We might talk in a Weberian sense, for example, of the 'office of the chief accountant,' referring both to the job or position filled by someone carrying the title of 'chief accountant,' to the department administered or managed by that person to execute the functions of the office, and the physical space in which they work.

- The defining feature of bureaucracy is that the authority of office holders derives from their offices (formal job titles) and not from their personal characteristics, charisma, or status. Within a bureaucracy, a rationally devised set of formal rules determines the functions, legal competence, and authority associated with each office. These are determined according to rational criteria of efficiency and effectiveness rather than by tradition and they are completely independent of who might occupy the office at any particular time.

- A central characteristic of bureaucracy is the strict separation of the rational work of the organization from the personal lives of its members. The single most important criterion for Weber was that posts should be filled according to rational criteria of ability, wherever possible demonstrated through competitive exams and technical qualifications. Personal qualities, social status, and connections have no place in a Weberian bureaucracy. There should also be a clear separation of the office from the ownership of the organization and of office work from personal life. To protect the office from personal interference, office holders should be full-time employees on pensionable salaries with opportunities for promotion and rights of tenure, strictly subject at work to the rules and regulations of the bureaucracy, but completely free outside work to live their own lives as they choose.

- Other distinguishing factors of bureaucracy include a clear hierarchy, with the relationships between offices and the authority of one over another clearly defined, and written sets of rules, norms, and procedures both for the organization as a whole and for each of its offices. One reason for having a physical office was to provide a repository for these reference manuals.

Weber noted that the pure bureaucratic form had emerged gradually and that many largely bureaucratic organizations still contained personal or traditional elements. Appointments to offices, for example, were rarely made on purely rational grounds. In its pure or 'monocratic' form, however, he considered bureaucracy 'superior to any other form [of organization] in precision, in stability, in the stringency of its discipline, and in its reliability. It thus makes possible a particularly high degree of calculability of results for the heads of the organisation and for those acting in relation to it. It is finally superior both in intensive efficiency and in the scope of its operations, and is formally capable of application to all kinds of administrative tasks.'

The other great advocate of modern bureaucratic management was Henri Fayol, a French mining engineer who spent most of his career as the managing director of a large iron and steel company. In 1916, turned seventy and approaching retirement, Fayol published a long paper on 'Administration industrielle et générale', subsequently reissued as a book and eventually published in English in 1949 as *General and Industrial Management*. Based largely on his own experience and on the application of general engineering principles to the problem of management, this set out fourteen principles of management:

1. Division of work.
2. Authority and responsibility. A good manager combines official authority, derived from his office, with personal authority, based on his skills, experience, moral worth, etc.
3. Worker discipline in the face of authority. Again, discipline is partly a requirement of the organization but should also be earned by the managers.
4. Unity of command, or a clear hierarchical structure.
5. Unity of direction, across the organization.
6. Subordination of individual interests to the general interest, based on fairness and consent as well as supervision.
7. Remuneration that is fair and tailored to the task and circumstances.
8. Centralization or decentralization, according to circumstances.
9. A scalar chain of authority, which does not, however, preclude communications across the hierarchy. Problems should be solved in a timely and efficient manner, but direct interactions between subordinates should always be authorized by their line managers.
10. Order: both 'a place for each and each one in his place' and 'the right man in the right place'.

11. Equity in how people are treated, combining kindliness with justice.

12. Stability of tenure of personnel.

13. Initiative, at all levels, within the limits of discipline.

14. Esprit de corps: harmony, union, and commonality of purpose.

Although their intellectual origins are completely different, there is a considerable overlap between Fayol's principles of management and Weber's characterization of rational bureaucracy. The main difference is that Fayol, as a practising manager, builds in more flexibility, e.g. in remuneration, and finds more room for the human side of management.

Dimensions of management

Historians of management generally distinguish between two different approaches to the challenges it poses. One approach is rational. The organization is seen as in some sense a machine, and the principal task of management as to design, engineer, and maintain that machine. Workers, in this approach, are seen either as simple cogs in the machine or as atomized individuals on the economic model, motivated primarily by financial self-interest. The other approach is variously described as human, organic, or normative. The organization is seen as a living organism bound together by personal relationships, and the workers are seen as having complex and interconnected needs and motivations. The principal task of management, in this approach, is to release the human potential of the workers so that the organization can benefit precisely from the fact that they are *not* mere cogs in a machine or atomized self-interested utility maximizers.

Within this scheme, bureaucracy is generally taken as a paradigm of rational management. Weber himself described the bureaucratic organization as a machine and saw the benefits of bureaucracy as lying in the removal of the distorting effects of personal and interpersonal relationships from organizational decision making. Elsewhere, adapting Tönnies's distinction between *Gemeinschaft* and *Gesellschaft*, he distinguished between associative (*Vergesellschaftung*) and communal (*Vergemeinschaftung*) forms of social relationship, based respectively on mutual self-interest and strong personal ties. Weberian bureaucracy, in this context, is clearly built on an associative model.

For much of the 20th century, this scheme works quite well. It tends, however, to conflate two slightly different dimensions, and so leads to some confusion, especially when we look at the debates of contemporary management. For while bureaucracy almost always has machine-like properties, the developed form of bureaucracy that dominated 20th-century management practice relied as much on communal as on associative relationships. The theoretical rationale may have been based on mutual self-interest, but the practical morality of bureaucratic organizations, like that of the hierarchical societies in which they were set, was based on the suppression of self-interest in favour of a shared sense of duty to the community as a whole. In this respect Fayol's model, emphasizing the subordination of individual interests, equity, and esprit de corps, gives a clearer picture of how bureaucracies work in practice. Moreover, when bureaucracies came in for heavy criticism later in the century, a major thrust of that criticism was that they removed individual responsibility and smothered individual enterprise. The 21st-century emphasis on enterprise and entrepreneurial management represents both a rejection of the mechanical rigidity of bureaucracy and, at the same time, a reaffirmation of self-interest.

In the following chapters I shall structure a discussion of management theory and practice around three tendencies rather than the usual two: a *rationalizing* tendency, epitomized by scientific management, management science, and management by objectives; a *socializing* tendency, epitomized by the human relations movement, the management of corporate culture, and management as leadership; and an *individualizing* tendency, epitomized by entrepreneurial management and performance incentives.

Weber said of his analysis of authority types that 'The idea that the whole of concrete historical reality can be exhausted in the conceptual scheme about to be developed is as far from the author's thoughts as anything could be.' The structure adopted here is more pragmatic still. The aim is simply to emphasize particular aspects of management in an ordered and, I hope, helpful fashion, not to provide a classification of any kind. All three aspects can be found in almost any contemporary organization and, as our review of management practice in Chapter 2 will have indicated, in the work of any manager.

Chapter 4
Rationalizing management

Alongside the principles of management summarized in the last chapter, Henri Fayol also offered a definition of management as comprising five logically and sequentially related elements:

1. Forecasting and planning: working out objectives and how to meet them;

2. Organization design and the assembly of staff and resources;

3. Command, or the direction of activity;

4. Coordination between the different activities;

5. Control, requiring a programme of monitoring, inspection, and corrective action where needed.

This definition has stood the test of time. It remains influential today. What it captures, however, is a distinctively engineering view of management. Charged with producing a particular product or output, an engineer will design, operate, and maintain a machine, building into it coordination and control mechanisms to ensure its smooth running according to the original calibrations. Fayol was, of course, an engineer by training, a graduate of the prestigious École Nationale Supérieure des Mines, and most of the industrial managers of the late 19th and early to mid 20th centuries came from similar backgrounds. Whereas Fayol was acutely conscious of the human dimension of management, however, and of the value it could bring, many of these engineer-managers were more concerned to eliminate it. This was particularly the case in America, where poor working conditions and a reliance on immigrant labour forces, perceived as combining un-American habits of beer drinking with un-American ideas of socialism, led in the late 19th century to escalating confrontations between employers and workers. The result was a movement which became known first as systematic management and later as scientific management, after a seminal work published in 1911 by Frederick Winslow Taylor, like Fayol a steel industry engineer-manager.

Scientific management

Taylor and his followers believed that most of the problems of industrial management could be solved by the application of scientific principles to the design and specification of jobs and organizations. Part of their aim was to remove inefficiencies. Part of it was to replace the antagonistic relationships of mistrust between workers and managers with agreements based on rational consensus, very much on the rational-bureaucratic model that would be outlined a few years later by Weber. The starting point was the assumption of financial self-interest. Owners wanted to maximize profits, workers wanted to maximize wages, and both therefore had a rational self-interest in the most efficient system possible.

Taylor suggested that the first stage in maximizing efficiency was a work-study or time-and-motion exercise designed to calculate how the work could be most efficiently carried out. This involved the analysis of different possible divisions of labour into specialized tasks, the optimization of the tools and machines, and the optimization of the physical movements required to operate them, assuming workers well suited to the specialized tasks concerned. The optimized system would then be codified so as to become a standard requirement, to be implemented with absolute regularity, so that the whole workplace operated as a machine. Workers would be selected with the skills and strengths to perform each specialized task, and trained to follow the standard procedures. They would be fairly paid for what was scientifically established to be a reasonable level of performance (assuming they were well suited to the tasks), with incentive pay introduced to encourage over-performance and punish underperformance. Both owners and employees would benefit.

Taylor's recipe could be applied to the simplest of tasks. He gave examples of shovelling and bricklaying that showed them to be far more open to improvement than anyone might have imagined. And he used baseball as an illustration of one activity that had been painstakingly analysed, using scientific reasoning to enhance performance. The recipe could also be applied to much more complicated, mechanized operations, and even to management itself. The primary role of management in Taylor's system was to design, implement, and oversee operations, very much on the engineering model, but management was also part of the machine. A key feature of scientific management was a much greater and more direct involvement of managers in the work process than was then normal, as the analysis of processes and the selection of workers were seen as ongoing, not one-off, activities, aimed at constant improvement. Taylor also suggested that management itself could be analysed in much the same way as manual work, being scientifically divided into specialist functions very much as in Weber's account of the ideal bureaucracy.

Taylor's writings and the writings of associates such as Harrington Emerson and Henry Gantt (creator of the Gantt chart, still today a standard tool of project management) were enormously influential at the time and have remained so ever since. Scientific management principles haven't always been applied in quite the spirit intended. Many employers, for example, used time-and-motion studies to increase workloads without providing any corresponding rewards. Workers might have their pay docked for failing to meet targets, but get little or no additional pay for exceeding them. In the manufacturing industry the use of mechanized production lines, pioneered at Ford around the same time as Taylor's ideas were becoming fashionable, achieved massive efficiency increases by imposing work rates and routines, effectively by physical force. The workers were compelled to operate at the speed of the line. The application of scientific management was also tied up with battles between employers and trade unions. Employers, guided by engineer-managers, used the prospects of enhanced earnings from more efficient processes to entice workers out of their unions, while the unions vigorously resisted all attempts to increase work quotas.

Over forty years after Taylor's death, in 1959, the British movie *I'm All Right, Jack*, starring Peter Sellers as a trade union shop steward, brought time-and-motion studies and the politics surrounding them to the attention of a general audience. As a theoretical approach scientific management had by then been long out of fashion, but the basic thinking behind it and the technologies it advanced were firmly implanted in management practice. Indeed, their influence was still growing: what was old hat in the large manufacturing corporations of the United States was only then gaining a foothold in smaller firms outside America. Since then, theoretical fashions have continued to come and go, but engineered work processes designed and overseen by specialist managerial functions have remained a constant feature of management practice. So too has the challenge of managing the tensions that result, when workers see efficiency enhancements less as the product of rational consensus and more as an imposition designed to exploit them.

Management science and systems engineering

One of the early triumphs of scientific management had been its adoption by the newly created Harvard Business School, in 1908, as the basis for professional management education. Underlying this move were two ideas that were to become increasingly important in the second half of the century. One was that managers should be university-trained experts in their field. The other was that this training should rest on an academically respectable base. Harvard used case study teaching methods adapted from law, in which students argued about what should be done or decided in real business situations, but it was mechanical engineering that provided the academic grounding.

Although many of the larger American universities opened schools of business or commerce in the late 19th and early 20th centuries, the numbers they trained were relatively small. The big explosion in numbers came in the decades following the Second World War, and at that stage the schools naturally built their legitimacy on the science and engineering of the period, in particular those developed in government laboratories during the war and in the Cold War period that followed. The new approach was called management science.

The key engineering discipline underlying this new approach was systems engineering. This was allied to the development of data-processing technologies (the first business computers were developed in the 1950s, and by the 1970s they were becoming commonplace) and the mathematical techniques of operations research: linear and non-linear programming, network analysis, queuing theory, simulation techniques, decision analysis, etc. Between them, these techniques opened up the possibility of taking scientific management a stage further, with much more sophisticated and scientific forecasting methods, detailed analysis that was no longer dependent simply on observation, and greatly enhanced systems of monitoring and control. In the 1960s and 1970s they became the recognized basis, together with finance and statistics, of management education.

This proved to be a passing fad. The mathematics of linear programming, for example, was of little practical use to the ordinary manager. Moreover, as the demand for business school degrees grew (and educational standards generally arguably fell), it quickly became apparent that management science was simply too difficult for most students. In business and public sector organizations it was always treated as a specialist staff function, providing analytical support for the design of operations, rather than as a function of line management. By the 1980s it had become a minority specialism in management degrees, and it remains so today. Systems engineering, similarly, has become a functional specialism rather than a general management tool.

Where the growth of management science has impacted significantly on management practice, however, is through a renewed emphasis on more 'scientific' approaches, captured in a range of techniques that are not necessarily scientifically based but are justified through a general appeal to rationality and efficiency. In the remainder of this chapter we shall explore some of the most influential of these techniques.

Management by objectives

One of the earliest and most influential of the new techniques was *management by objectives* (MBO), expounded by Peter Drucker in the mid 1950s and codified in the form of a 'how to manage' manual by George Odiorne in 1965. Drucker was by far the most influential of popular management writers in the second half of the 20th century and is often credited with inventing the scientific discipline of management. His approach was not unlike Fayol's, in that it was based on general rational principles allied to observation and common sense rather than on any particular theory, and like Fayol he summarized management as comprising five elements. In Drucker's case these were:

1. Objective setting;
2. Organization;

3. Motivation and communication;
4. Measurement and analysis;
5. Self-development and self-control.

Management by objectives takes what is effectively the scientific management model of objective setting, work analysis, target setting, measurement, and control, and applies it specifically to the work of managers as well as to the management of workers. Frederick Taylor's assumption of economic self-interest is, however, replaced by a general view of managers (and workers) as autonomous, responsible rational beings. When Drucker set out his principles of management by objectives, he was strongly impressed by recent developments in social psychology, to be considered in the next chapter, which emphasized the rich potential of human beings and their capacity for self-motivation. He later came to the slightly different view that people are different and have different motivations, and that an important part of the job of a manager is to find the appropriate way of motivating the people reporting to him. Once people are correctly motivated, however, they will want to improve their own performance as well as those of their own reports. In Drucker's model, much more clearly than in Taylor's, performance measurement becomes a means of self-improvement and self-control.

Management by objectives works by setting clear objectives for every manager (and every worker) throughout the organization. The process starts at the top, and it is essential that all the objectives are aligned, but at each level of the hierarchy managers work out with their superiors and subordinates the specific objectives and performance targets for each managerial unit. These targets might be demanding but they should be realistic. They should state clearly the areas in which contributions are not expected as well as those in which they are, and they should include clear statements of what each unit can expect to receive from others. As in Taylor's theoretical model, though not as in its

44

typical applications, the setting of targets is meant to be a consensual process, but in Drucker's model the primary responsibility for drawing up objectives lies with the manager responsible for delivering on them.

The second aspect of management by objectives is a detailed performance measurement system—not necessarily strictly quantitative, but rational and unambiguous—covering all the factors that contribute to achieving the agreed objectives. Crucially, these detailed measurements should go to the unit manager, not to his superior. They should, in Drucker's words, be 'the means of self-control, not a tool of control from above.' Managers are accountable for meeting their units' overall objectives, but they should have autonomy over how this is done.

Management by objectives has been most famously and most rigorously applied by the Hewlett Packard Corporation as the central feature of 'the HP Way', which stresses the self-motivation and creativity of employees and affords them considerable autonomy, while imposing clear and very demanding objectives. As with management science, however, the requirements of theory have generally proved too demanding for practice. Most applications have been much less rigorous, with only vague objectives, limited or non-existent feedback mechanisms, and a greater emphasis on control than on autonomy and self-control. In the long run, the most enduring legacy of the approach has probably been a reinforcement of the Taylorist elements of performance measurement and control applied at management levels.

Business strategy and strategic planning

A key part of any system of rational or scientific management is setting the objectives for the organization as a whole. Traditionally described as *business policy*, this received relatively little systematic attention before the post-war period. As with policy making in the public sphere, policy making in organizations was thought to be a matter of judgement based largely on experience and insight. The Second World War, however, focused attention on the possibilities of using scientific methods to support *strategic* planning. The policy issue here had been whether to go to war or not, and for the leaders of military organizations it was imposed and could be taken for granted. The strategic issue with which they were concerned was how to win.

Transferred to a business context, there is much in the policy area that might be debated—the balance between profit maximization and social responsibility, for example—but the main problem facing senior managers is not whether to make a profit but how. In the 1960s a new management discipline emerged called *business strategy*, and from the 1970s through to the 1990s it was to be the single most dominant management discourse. Strategy was, by definition, important. It was also technical (without necessarily being too technically difficult), masculine, and to do with controlling rather than being controlled. Everybody wanted a bit of it.

The new discipline adopted the basic structure of rational management. Policy objectives having been set or assumed, the task was to gather information, analyse it, make a rational decision, and implement that decision. Business strategy focused mainly on the analysis and decision making, implementation being dismissed as not really strategic. Ideologically, it drew on the achievements of management science, but in practice it used much simpler, cruder techniques of rationalization. Thus the information search was rationalized in the form of what became known as a PEST or STEP analysis. Following the general principle that a successful business strategy should be a rational response to the business's environment, this simply divides the external environment into four components: Political, Economic, Social, and Technological.

The dominant analytical tool was the SWOT analysis, which again offered a simple classification of relevant internal and external factors into Strengths, Weaknesses, Opportunities, and Threats, presented in a simple 2×2 matrix. The dominant decision tools were two more 2×2 matrices. Dating back to the 1950s, Igor Ansoff's growth matrix (growth as a policy objective was almost universally assumed in this period), known more usually as the *Ansoff matrix*, suggested a choice between different combinations of new or existing markets and new or existing products, the key decision criterion being to match the business's skills and resources to the market environment. The Boston Consulting Group (BCG) matrix, or *Boston box*, provided a tool for classifying subsidiary product units of a diversified business according to their market growth rates and the relative market share held, and a recipe based on a statistical analysis of company performance for choosing which to invest in and which to divest from. Illustrations of these various models are given in Figure 2.

Although they were rooted in a mix of theoretical and empirical insights, these techniques were taught and used—and are still taught and used—more as conceptual frameworks than as rigorous analytical tools. What they did, however, was to give generations of new managers a common language. Few business school graduates could do a good strategic analysis, and although they also learnt the financial language of net present value and return on investment, few could combine this necessary quantitative analysis with the strategy models. Like management science, formal strategic analysis was quickly delegated to more highly trained staff specialists in strategic planning offices. But anyone with a management education could talk the language of strategy, and they could provide rationalized accounts of their strategic decisions.

In the 1980s and 1990s, these simple analytical tools were supplemented and to some extent replaced by tools based on the emerging discipline of industrial organization economics.

	Positive	Negative
Internal	STRENGTHS	WEAKNESSES
External	OPPORTUNITIES	THREATS

(b) Ansoff matrix

	Existing products	New products
Existing markets	MARKET PENETRATION	PRODUCT DEVELOPMENT
New markets	MARKET DEVELOPMENT	DIVERSIFICATION

(c) Boston box

	Low market share	High market share
High market growth	QUESTION MARKS	STARS
Low market growth	DOGS	CASH COWS

2. Early strategic management models

Traditional economic price theory, based on assumptions of perfect information leading to perfect markets, predicts that all firms in all industries will make standard profits. (Strictly speaking, it actually predicts that there will be no firms and indeed no money, but industrial organization economists set this aside and start from the more practical assumption that firms do exist.) If profits in any industry were to rise above a standard level, new firms would move in, increasing competition and bringing profits back to the standard level. If they were to fall, firms would move out. And if two firms in the same industry earned different profits, the more profitable would drive out the less. It is clear, however, that some industries and some firms within each industry are in practice more profitable than others. In economic language, real industrial markets, unlike many commodity and financial markets, are not efficient, and there are mobility barriers between industries. A firm cannot just move from growing oranges to making computers, at no cost and in no time.

Building on the study of mobility barriers, Harvard Business School economist Michael Porter introduced in the 1980s a simple *Five forces* model for analysing market inefficiencies at the industry level and a *Generic strategies* model that cast strategic decision making as a choice between lowest-cost and product-differentiation strategies on one dimension, and a broad or narrow market orientation on the other (see Figure 3). Other industrial economists, meanwhile, were focusing on the link between strategy and a firm's resources, and Porter soon extended his own repertoire to include a value chain model of resource analysis, providing a conceptual framework for the implementation of a generic strategy by thoroughly implementing and tightly coordinating objectives across the organization. Shortly afterwards, Gary Hamel and C. K. Prahalad provided another influential application of the resource-based approach to strategy in the form of their *Core competence* concept, suggesting that a successful company should be built on a distinctive framework of skills and technologies that penetrated every aspect of its activity and could be used as the basis for a range of different businesses (see Figure 4).

Porter's work gave strategic management a new scientific legitimacy and while few managers understand it (many strategic management textbooks completely ignore its economic origins)

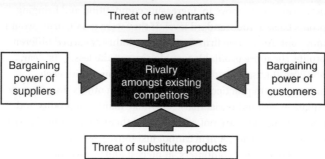

(a) The five forces on an industry

Threat of new entrants

Bargaining power of suppliers

Rivalry amongst existing competitors

Bargaining power of customers

Threat of substitute products

(b) Generic strategies

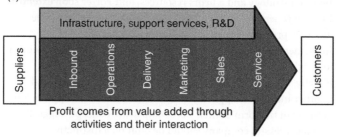

	Lowest cost advantage	Differentiation advantage
Broad scope	COST LEADERSHIP	DIFFERENTIATION
Narrow scope	COST FOCUS	DIFFERENTIATION FOCUS

(c) Value chain

Infrastructure, support services, R&D

Suppliers

Inbound | Operations | Delivery | Marketing | Sales | Service

Customers

Profit comes from value added through activities and their interaction

3. Porter's strategy models

the basic models have, like their predecessors, become a staple of management discourse. Fighting against this stream of analytical rationalizing, one influential writer, Henry Mintzberg, has argued persistently that management is more a craft than a science: that

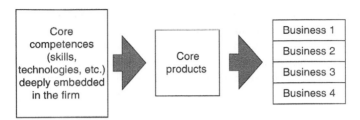

4. Core competence

it is best learnt by using theory to reflect on your practical experience, not by following prescriptive models; and that strategies are as much emergent as planned. He has been fighting a losing battle.

Decision making

One aspect of rational management that received a lot of academic attention in the post-war period was decision making itself. This hasn't found its way into management practice to anything like the extent that the analytical tools of business strategy have, but it has been addressed by some of the leading social scientists of the era. While management scientists developed formal decision-analysis techniques in an attempt to minimize the role of human judgement, social scientists looked more closely at what that judgement entailed, and at the limits of rationality in human decision processes.

The starting point here was Herbert Simon's observation, noted in Chapter 1, that a manager could not take account of all possible information, could not forecast the future or even assign probabilities to possible alternatives, and could not conduct every possible analysis, but had to 'satisfice' (from 'satisfy' and 'suffice'). The rational response to radical information uncertainty and limited mental ability was to seek good-enough decisions rather than perfect ones. Simon's approach was highly rational. He won the Nobel Prize for Economics and his demonstration of the rationality of satisficing took the form of a highly mathematical analysis. One way to address the managerial problem, he thought, was to routinize as many decisions as possible, avoiding duplications of analysis and leaving managers free to concentrate on those issues that needed to be addressed afresh, and he looked to information technologies and management science to achieve this. He also looked to these technologies to provide support for the decisions that couldn't be routinized. He insisted, however, that decision making could never be fully rationalized. Managers were at best only 'boundedly rational,' and human judgement would always be a factor in their choices.

This insight was developed in several ways. In 1959 the political scientist Charles Lindblom drew on it to distinguish between the ideal of rational-comprehensive decision making and the more practical alternative of decision making by successive incremental comparisons, or 'the science of muddling through'. Simon's colleague, James March, noted that in an organizational setting decision making would be compromised not only by the cognitive limits invoked by Simon but also by the entry into judgements of irrational personal preferences and, especially, of political considerations. Writing with Michael Cohen and Johan Olsen in 1972, he described organizations as 'collections of choices looking for problems, issues and feelings looking for decision situations in which they might be aired, solutions looking for issues to which they might be the answer, and decision-makers looking for work.' The need to make a decision, they suggested, becomes a 'garbage can' into which all sorts of personal, political, and organizational elements get thrown.

Consistent with a rationalizing approach to management, the garbage can model was presented in the form of a computer simulation, but its main impact was to stress the limits of rationalizing models and open up the exploration of the social, political, and social-psychological dimensions of the subject.

Moving into the 1980s, psychologist Irving Janis took things in the opposite direction. In 1972 he had published a classical study, *Victims of Groupthink*, of how group dynamics and in particular a desire to avoid conflict and reach consensus lead groups to overlook key considerations and suspend critical rational evaluation, resulting in blatantly irrational decisions. *Crucial Decisions*, published in 1989, offered not only a comprehensive theory of decision making but a long list of prescriptions as to how the irrational elements of decision making could be controlled and eliminated. Just like the strategy literature emerging in the same period, it combined rationalistic recipes for management success with a suitably scientific rhetoric (the prescriptions were actually labelled 'hypotheses,' though they were not hypotheses at all, taking the standard form of 'in this situation managers should do this'), but without expecting the reader to look too closely into the relation between what was proposed and the science that might or might not underlie it.

The main scientific advance in our understanding of decision making in this period takes us back to the cognitive aspects explored by Herbert Simon and has come from cognitive psychologists Daniel Kahnemann and Amos Tversky. *Prospect theory*, for which Kahneman received a Nobel Prize (Tversky had by then died), operates in a relatively narrow context in which it can be assumed that the mathematical probabilities of different outcomes are known. Based on decision-making experiments, it explores the ways in which people systematically make irrational choices as a result of inbuilt cognitive biases and heuristics (shorthand ways of thinking), corresponding to the satisficing modes of reasoning people adopt to cope with some of the problems identified by Simon. It turns out, for example, that people systematically treat gains and losses differently, respond differently to situations presented as threats from those presented as opportunities, and generally respond to risk in inconsistent but predictable ways. They also overestimate the value of private information, have an inherent conservative bias, etc.

Mathematically formulated and based on narrow assumptions, Kahneman and Tversky's work has so far been more influential in economics than management, but it has gradually found its way into management thinking and looks likely to be influential in the future, especially following a more user-friendly account by Kahneman in the form of a recent intellectual autobiography.

Contingency theory and organization design

One of Peter Drucker's early observations was that while the simple top-down organizational and decision-making structures associated with scientific management might work for a steel producer, they did not always work in the more diversified American corporations that emerged in the early part of the 20th century. This phenomenon was explored by historian Alfred Chandler, who argued in his 1962 book *Strategy and Structure* that the structure of organizations followed the strategies they chose, and that a key part of the manager's role was to design an appropriate structure for the strategy.

Meanwhile Tom Burns and G. M. Stalker, who had been studying the process of technological innovation in smaller firms, identified two 'ideal type' organizations. One, which they labelled 'mechanistic', corresponded to traditional Weberian bureaucracy and appeared well suited to stable conditions but resistant to change. The other, termed 'organismic', was less hierarchical, more flexible and interdependent, and held together more by a shared commitment than by loyalty and obedience, and appeared well suited to innovation and change.

A few years later, in 1967, Paul Lawrence and Jay Lorsch suggested on the basis of a study of a cross-section of American firms that successful firms needed to combine an effective differentiation between their different functional units with an effective integration of these units. The more uncertain the environment in which a firm operated, they argued, the greater the degree of differentiation that was required and the greater the corresponding need for integrative mechanisms.

All these approaches to organization design were forms of 'contingency theory,' which can be seen as a rational response to the limitations of simple rational models. If these models do not always seem to work in practice, we postulate it is because they rest on assumptions that do not always hold in practice. The aim of the contingency theorist is to identify through observation and analysis what factors vary, in successful organizations, with what conditions. Practising managers can then draw on contingency theories to guide their decision making: if you are faced with a complex, fast-changing environment, for example, don't go for a rigid, uniform, undifferentiated hierarchy.

Contingency theory was not restricted to the question of organization design. Fred Fiedler, for example, developed a contingency theory of leadership, proposing different leadership styles (task motivated or relation motivated) for different sets of circumstances. Victor Vroom proposed a contingency theory of decision making, distinguishing between different forms of consultation and participation and developing a model to prescribe which approach should be used under which organizational conditions. It was in organization design that it made the greatest impact, however, especially when the different research streams were brought together by Henry Mintzberg, showing here his rational aspect. Mintzberg developed a model (Figure 5) that classified organizations according to five, later six, types or, more accurately, tendencies. Each was characterized by a particular balance of power between the different parts of the organization, a coordinating mechanism reflecting the interests of the dominant part, and a characteristic pattern of centralization and decentralization. And each was associated with particular environmental conditions and a particular approach to strategy.

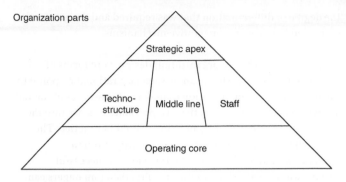

Organization parts

Structural configurations

Configuration	Coordinating mechanism	Dominant pull in organization
Simple structure	Direct supervision	Strategic apex
Machine bureaucracy	Standardization of work processes	Technostructure (work design and operations)
Professional bureaucracy	Standardization of skills	Operating core (professionals)
Multidivisional form	Standardization of outputs	Middle line managers
Adhocracy	Mutual adjustment	Staff (infrastructure and systems)
Missionary	Standardization of norms	Ideology (organization as a whole)

5. Mintzberg's model of organization structure

The logic underlying Mintzberg's model was that while there were many possible combinations of environmental, strategic, and organizational variables, relatively few of them would be coherent enough to be stable, and businesses would tend to fall into those patterns that were. His model helps managers to understand and analyse their organizations and also to focus on what may need attention, for optimization in any one direction will inevitably produce compromises in others. Contingency theory from this perspective is as much about identifying the weaknesses of any approach to management as it is about exploiting its strengths.

Business process re-engineering and human resource management

While many of the approaches described in this chapter sought to provide an improved rational foundation for management, they lacked the ideological rationalism of the pioneers of scientific management. That returned, however, in the early 1990s. Michael Hammer, Thomas Davenport, and their associates argued that because most organizations had evolved gradually they had become weighed down with activities and processes that no longer added value. Many had introduced new information technologies, but they had done so to automate old and redundant processes. What they should be doing was *business process re-engineering*: looking afresh at their entire business processes and rebuilding them, along the lines of scientific management but in the light of current technological capabilities, and especially of computerized information systems, to realign them with objectives and cut out the accumulated inefficiencies.

In many cases these criticisms were well founded. Both private and public sector organizations had responded to the growing complexity of their environments by taking on more managers and analysts. This had resulted in greater problems of coordination, which they had reacted to by employing more managers and analysts. Wedded to a traditional bureaucratic model in which they sought to provide managers with long-term careers and not just short-term jobs, many had also been reluctant to close down activities that were no longer central to their objectives. Business process re-engineering provided a timely corrective and a much-needed efficiency boost to American and European firms at a time of increasing global competition. On the other hand, many babies were thrown out with the bathwater, and the managers who remained were often left with impossible workloads as they struggled to fill the gaps created. A recent study of organizational restructuring in Britain, America, and Japan found organizations that were rationalized but also dangerously dehumanized, with middle managers routinely facing unsustainably long hours, limited career prospects, and high stress levels.

While part of what drove the business process re-engineering movement was a passionate belief in rationality and efficiency, part of it was an attempt by a large but strategically marginalized group of information systems experts to raise their status and take their place at the heart of business strategy. A similar move also lies behind our last example of rationalizing tendencies, the growth of human resource management, which occurred in the same period. Although the pioneers of scientific management laid great stress on the selection, training, and performance appraisal of employees, this part of their prescription was widely neglected. The personnel function, as it came to be known, was dominated through much of the 20th century by routine administration such as payroll on the one hand and industrial relations—negotiating with the trade unions—on the other.

With the erosion of trade union power in the Reagan–Thatcher era, however, and the increasing automation of payroll, personnel departments looked to play a more active role in both strategy and the management process generally. They began to advance psychological testing techniques for employee selection and performance measurement techniques for their appraisal; and to take responsibility for the training and development of the workforce, identifying leadership potential, and managing people out of the organization as well as into and around it. In this last capacity, indeed, they were important players in the business process re-engineering movement, providing a rational basis for fitting people to tasks and managing large-scale redundancy programmes. They also brought a rational approach to the protection of employees, with formal systems to counter bullying and harassment and to protect people from unfair or personally motivated dismissal.

The term 'human resource management' carries an interesting mix of connotations. The 'human' emphasizes the fact that employees are people and not just cogs in a machine, with needs to be considered and rights to be protected. The 'resource' suggests that like other resources—material or financial—the people are basically there to be exploited. The most significant impact of human resource management, however, has been to provide a rational framework for interpersonal relationships. While managers still manage, and are managed, on a personal level (and the chief executive's nephew might still get a job or at least an internship in preference to others more able), this now takes place within a structure of formal human resource procedures.

Chapter 5
Socializing management

How you approach the task of rationalizing management depends largely on your view of human motivation. Frederick Taylor and the advocates of scientific management shared the common assumption of American managers of their time that workers were inherently lazy and selfish, but thought that they could also be motivated by money, and could be rationally persuaded to go along with anything that gave them more money. For Peter Drucker, money was only a small part of the equation. He held, following the psychological research of his day, that different people began with different motivations. With the right encouragement, however, he thought that all could be motivated towards self-improvement. Henri Fayol, meanwhile, saw potential in the socially motivating force of esprit de corps.

These differences have a cultural element. The value of self-improvement, in particular, is deeply ingrained in American culture, where it can be traced back to the popular writings of Benjamin Franklin in the 18th century. The idea that people might be motivated by social ties, on the other hand, though it came naturally to the Frenchman, Fayol, was treated more suspiciously in America. In the business context, especially, social bonding was associated with trade unions, and trade unions (themselves often influenced by European ideas) were associated with a conspiracy to avoid work. Indeed, while scientific management took its legitimacy from rational engineering, its popularity owed much more to its union-busting potential.

Not all Americans took this view, however. Alongside the rationalizing tendencies in American management discussed in the last chapter there was also an ongoing exploration of how the potential of self-improvement could be harnessed through socializing forces of one kind or another, and it was the work of American psychologists in mid century that brought this socializing tendency to bear systematically on management practice. One of the most influential writings in this context was Douglas McGregor's book, *The Human Side of Management*. Published in 1960, this introduced the terminology of Theory X and Theory Y, which provides a convenient starting point for our discussion in this chapter.

Theory X and Theory Y

McGregor suggested that any manager brings to his task a set of assumptions about the attitudes and motivations of the people working for him, together with a related set of assumptions about how they should be managed. Traditional management practices, he suggested, were based on a set of assumptions he labelled Theory X:

1. The average human being has an inherent dislike of work and will avoid it if he can.

2. Because of this human characteristic of dislike of work, most people must be coerced, controlled, directed, threatened with punishment to get them to put forth adequate effort toward the achievement of organizational objectives. The dislike of work is so strong that even the promise of rewards is not generally enough to overcome it.

3. The average human being prefers to be directed, wishes to avoid responsibility, has relatively little ambition, wants security above all.

This theory, he suggested, was not entirely without foundation. But the psychological research accumulated over the preceding twenty years suggested that it was misleading in many ways. As an alternative, not yet fully proven but more consistent with recent findings, he suggested Theory Y:

1. The expenditure of physical or mental effort in work is as natural as play or rest. Depending upon controllable conditions, work may be a source of satisfaction or a source of punishment.

2. External control and the threat of punishment are not the only means for bringing about effort toward organizational objectives. Man will exercise self-direction and self-control in the service of objectives to which he is committed.

3. Commitment to objectives is a function of rewards associated with their achievement. The most significant of such rewards, e.g. the satisfaction of ego and self-actualization needs, can be direct products of efforts directed towards organizational objectives.

4. The average human being learns, under proper conditions, not only to accept but to seek responsibility.

5. The capacity to exercise a relatively high degree of imagination, ingenuity, and creativity in the solution of organizational problems is widely, not narrowly, distributed in the population.

6. Under the conditions of modern industrial life, the intellectual potentialities of the average human being are only partially utilized.

McGregor's proposal has several features of note. There is, first, something of the same belief in self-improvement that we saw in Drucker, linked here with the taking of responsibility and the exercise of creativity. There is the emphasis on human creativity itself, which was to be important for later management developments. And there is the core idea, the 'central principle' on McGregor's account, of the integration of individual and organizational goals. Management is not just about aligning the goals of the individual to those of the organization, as in Taylor's scientific management, but also about aligning the organization to the goals of the individual. The commitment of employees, which McGregor sees as essential for the success of the organization, has to be generated through social and interpersonal relationships and cannot be gained just by economic incentives.

Alternatives to coercion: betterment and paternalism

If we look back at traditional, pre-industrial approaches to management, we can see elements of both Theory X and Theory Y. The dominant mode may have been coercive, but there have always been enlightened employers who have taken a more positive view of their workers' attitudes and abilities and sought to gain their commitment by kindness and responsiveness. With the large-scale industrialization of the second half of the 19th century, sheer scale and the necessary resort to bureaucratic structures tended to depersonalize the organization, making it harder to manage in this way. Under conditions of coercion, control, and worker alienation, the assumptions of Theory X often became effectively self-fulfilling.

Again, though, there were exceptions, and while many employers saw their labourers as hopeless cases of moral degeneracy, some saw hope in moral reform. By improving living conditions, providing education and health care, libraries and social clubs, they thought that they could both fulfil their own moral responsibilities as (typically, Protestant Christian) employers and, by lifting their workers and their families out of the conditions of insanitary homes, alcoholism, and ignorance, create better, more reliable, and more productive workforces. By the 1890s, some companies, such as Cadbury and Lever Brothers in England and Pullman and N. O. Nelson in America, were building model villages to house their workforces, while many more were introducing more modest welfare or 'betterment' programmes.

These paternalistic approaches to management were not always well regarded, especially by rival employers who had no wish to spend their own money on such programmes, doubted if they would work anyway, and preferred to lay the blame for workers' bad habits on the workers themselves. Scientific management was, in general, a much more attractive route to follow, especially when shorn of some of its more positive and enabling aspects and reduced to a system of sophisticated coercion. More modest employee welfare programmes proved invaluable in countering the largely accurate public perception that the modern corporation was dehumanizing and lacked soul. These grew rapidly after the First World War and became the norm in the large 20th-century corporation. But for the first half of the century, at least, a more inclusive and socializing approach to management was restricted to relatively few companies, large or small.

The human relations movement

A more systematic adoption of socializing approaches to management had to wait until after the Second World War, but it rested on scientific developments made during the interwar years. This period saw the growth of interest in Freudian psychoanalysis and other psychodynamic approaches, and also in group psychology. The key figure in these developments was Elton Mayo, an Australian professor based at the Harvard Business School.

When he moved to Harvard in the 1920s, Mayo had been working mainly on the psychological problems associated with production line management, especially the problem of fatigue and how it could be mitigated (and productivity enhanced) by rest pauses. He also had a growing interest in clinical psychology and psychoanalysis, however, and was beginning to look at psychodynamic explanations of worker behaviour. And he was also interested in developments in sociology and anthropology.

At Harvard an ongoing study, characteristic of those carried out within the framework of scientific management, had been investigating the effects of lighting levels on worker productivity at the Hawthorne works of the Western Electric Company in Chicago. It had reached the puzzling conclusion that while output was generally the same regardless of lighting level, it went up whenever the level was changed, whether up or down. Mayo followed this up with a prolonged study of a group of workers assembling telephone relays, experimenting with various changes in working conditions and incentives. This study, which produced similarly puzzling results, was followed by a wider interview programme, which highlighted the importance of emotions, and by observations of workers in natural (i.e. not test) conditions, which showed them manipulating output according to their own social conventions, regardless of the incentive scheme in operation. Mayo's eventual conclusion was that output was determined less by working conditions or incentive systems than by the informal social pattern of the work group. Feelings mattered, and wherever managers took a personal interest in the workers, made them feel important, and generated a mutually supportive and cooperative environment, output was enhanced. Management, it seemed, was not about mechanical optimization processes but about leadership and team dynamics.

Mayo's conclusions were pulled together in 1933 in *The Human Problems of an Industrial Civilization* and again in *Management and the Worker* by two of his colleagues, Fritz Roethlisberger and William Dickson. Both books became bestsellers. Mayo's conclusions were given a further boost by the publication in 1938 of *The Functions of the Executive*, by businessman Chester Barnard. Based on practical experience rather than management science, this also stressed the importance of cooperation and mutual respect, in marked opposition to the established norm of management as control. The decade following the Second World War then witnessed an explosion of both academic research and industrial innovation within what became known as the 'human relations movement.'

On the research side, Rensis Likert demonstrated benefits from participative group management. Herbert Maslow proposed a hierarchy of needs, ranging from basic physiological needs up to self-actualization, and suggested that once a level of needs had been met, it ceased to act as a positive motivator. Frederick Herzberg, on rather more solid empirical ground, showed that the 'motivation' factors contributing to job satisfaction were different from the 'hygiene factors' whose absence contributed to job dissatisfaction, and argued on this basis that output would benefit from job enrichment, rather than from the job simplification recommended by scientific management. At the Tavistock Institute in London, Eric Trist and his colleagues combined the human relations perspective with the systems thinking then shaping management science approaches in their theory of work groups as 'socio-technical systems,' in which social-psychological and technical requirements are mutually interactive. Kurt Lewin's theory of group dynamics and Carl Rogers's developmental psychology were also influential on both management education and practice.

Several of these research programmes were closely linked with developments in management practice, and the movement quickly spawned a new industry of 'management consulting,' with consultants trained in the new techniques offering services in organizational development, work design, and industrial relations. Books describing the new approaches, including McGregor's *The Human Side of Enterprise*, had a broad popular appeal, and they quickly became a staple of management training and education.

From the beginning, however, they had their critics. The new 'science', which relied heavily on qualitative data and interpretative methods, and used only the simplest descriptive statistics, was too soft and woolly, too lacking in rigour, for the majority of business school faculty trained in economics, mathematics, or engineering. The Theory Y assumptions were met with deep scepticism, both by those accustomed to the individualistic and rationalistic assumptions of economics and scientific management and by hardened managers, whose more cynical view of employees proved self-fulfilling and self-reinforcing.

More fundamentally, while the human relations approach to management was attractive enough in the classroom, it was incredibly difficult to put into practice. It required not only a high level of interpersonal skills, but also great patience and a great investment of time, which few managers had, or could sustain, or could afford. The philosophy of human relations continues to influence management today, but it is honoured more in the breach than the observance.

Japanese management and organizational culture

While consultants and practitioners struggled to put human relations principles into practice, the emergence of serious competition to American and European multinationals from Japan in the 1970s suggested an alternative take on the problem of worker commitment. For while the large Japanese companies seemed to benefit from very high levels of employee commitment, this was not obviously achieved through inspirational leadership or empowering managers. On the contrary, Japanese firms were strongly hierarchical organizations, with many of the characteristics of traditional bureaucracy. They did, however, offer lifetime employment (albeit only for men—women were still expected, as they had been in Europe fifty years earlier, to resign on marriage) and comprehensive social welfare programmes, and they also bound their employees to the aims of the organization through very strong corporate cultures. In the early 1980s a rash of popular, practitioner-oriented books, mainly written by management consultants, extolled the virtues of corporate or organizational culture as a management tool.

Some of these books focused explicitly on the virtues of Japanese management. The most influential of these, both published in 1981 and instant bestsellers, were *The Art of Japanese Management*, by McKinsey consultants Richard Pascale and Anthony Athos, and *Theory Z: How American Business can Meet the Japanese Challenge*, by management professor Bill Ouchi. 'Theory Z' was Ouchi's recipe for how American companies might adopt and adapt some of the key features of Japanese management, and was presented as building on but further developing McGregor's Theory Y.

The most striking feature of Japanese management was the priority it gave to collective over individual values. Decision making was highly consensual, with no decision formally taken until all those affected and concerned had committed to it. This was accompanied by collective responsibility. There were no individual incentives, and although the basic structure was bureaucratic, teamwork was commonplace and cut across bureaucratic lines, as managers put together teams based on skills and personalities rather than job titles. There was a high level of trust between managers, and between workers and managers, and innovations were welcomed rather than rejected. The flexibility of the organization and the job security combined to allow people to experiment collectively with new ideas, without fear of short-term performance consequences.

All this was made possible by a setting in which people knew each other intimately and were motivated by common goals. Part of this came from lifetime employment. Part of it came from extensive company-specific training programmes. Part of it came from a caring and trusting environment, and from an interweaving of business and social life. Leisure was an extension of work, and the company acted as an extended family—to the detriment, often, of a manager's real family, who might see very little of him. At the centre was a strong set of corporate values, embodied in symbols, routines, and practices, and supporting a common understanding of what the company was about, where it was going, and how it was getting there: a strong organizational culture.

These explorations of Japanese management were quickly followed in 1982 by two books extolling the virtues of a strong corporate culture in American corporations: *Corporate Culture*, by Terrence Deal and Allan Kennedy, and the biggest seller of all, *In Search of Excellence*, by two more McKinsey consultants, Tom Peters and Robert Waterman. The following year, these were joined by yet another blockbuster, *The Change Masters*, by Harvard Business School's Rosabeth Moss Kanter.

The most influential of these books was *In Search of Excellence*. Drawing on studies of top-performing American corporations (where performance was assessed in terms of growth, financial returns, and, crucially, responsiveness or innovation) Peters and Waterman identified eight characteristics of excellence that appeared to distinguish these firms from their less successful competitors. Modelled on McKinsey's '7-S Framework' for business and organizational analysis, these combined organizational, strategic, and management elements. Key claims, for example, were that excellent firms were close to their customers and had a narrow strategic focus (they 'stuck to their knitting'). The management characteristics were, however, critical, and with some rearrangement they can be summarized as follows:

- A strong people orientation. Everybody is treated as part of the team and not just as an expendable or replaceable resource.

- Hands-on management, with a bias to action. Managers get involved, working with people to make things happen and find solutions. They don't just analyse and give instructions.

- Autonomy and entrepreneurship. People are encouraged to innovate and experiment, and to implement their proposals; failure is tolerated, and decision making is passed down the line.

- Flexibility and teamwork. The organization structure is seen as a resource, not a constraint. Issues are addressed through ad hoc teams, often constructed on a voluntary basis.

- Value driven. A clear and explicit value system running right through the company, communicating what the company stands for, what's excellent about it, and what it's trying to achieve.

Some of these characteristics reflected recognized good practice in a world still heavily influenced by Theory Y prescriptions. Others reflected observations that had clearly been interpreted in the light of Japanese management practices. For Peters and Waterman, the single most important element was the emphasis on culture and values, and they captured the rationale behind this in one of their eight characteristics: simultaneous loose–tight properties. The basic idea was that if you could use a very tight organizational culture to tie people into a clear direction and set of objectives, then you could dispense with more traditional control mechanisms and free them up to be innovative and creative, confident that this would work in the company's interests.

Immensely appealing as it was, this idea proved, like so many others, to be rather hard to put into practice. Peters and Waterman themselves noted that another characteristic of their excellent companies was exceptional leaders, many of whom had shaped their companies. Academic studies of organizational culture and change, which began around the same time, suggested that cultures were often closely associated with a founding figure, and were always deeply rooted in a company's history. As anthropological research suggested, culture and history were closely entwined, and changing a culture was no easy matter. It was not enough to change structures and systems, for so long as there were still embodiments of the old culture—in symbols, stories, routines, and so on—the organization would tend to fall back into its old patterns. Even when an inspired leader did manage to engineer a major change, it proved hard to sustain beyond his tenure.

Many of the ideas popularized at this time were, nevertheless, carried forward. Today's bureaucracies are much, much more flexible than their predecessors. Managers work more as a team, they treat their reports more as team members, and teamwork generally is more pervasive. Some companies use teams as a basic organizing device; others as a device for problem solving and innovation. Senior managers often recognize the importance of strong shared values, even if they cannot often create a value-driven culture. And the loose–tight formula is often applied at the project team level, where the challenge of the project itself can motivate a strong shared commitment.

Moreover, while older companies may struggle to change their cultures, many of the world's most exciting companies, still young enough to benefit from cultures built by their founders, are managed in a way that is recognizably related to Peters and Waterman's recipe: Apple, Google, Amazon, and Virgin, for example, all work on the loose–tight principle.

Finally, one aspect highlighted both by Peters and Waterman and by Kanter has also impacted in a rather different way. Entrepreneurial management has become very much part of the mainstream, but while companies like Google can use their socializing approach to management to capture its benefits for the firm, many organizations rely instead on a combination of old-fashioned controls and individualizing incentives. In the next chapter we turn to this individualizing tendency in management.

Chapter 6
Individualizing management

Although the scientific management of the early 20th century was based on what we would now term an economic model of the working man (*homo economicus*) as a self-seeking economic utility maximizer, this model was not then extended to managers. Workers were considered inherently lazy and self-interested beings who would perform satisfactorily only if given financial incentives, on the scientific management model, or if coerced, on the more popular model captured later by McGregor's Theory X. Managers, however, as members of the respectable middle classes, were assumed to be morally upright and socially responsible members of the community. This did not preclude financial self-interest, especially in the American context. Success, for Americans, was measured very largely in monetary terms. But even in America other things were assumed to matter too, and elsewhere they were dominant. Behind the interwar and post-war development of the human relations movement were the experiences of two world wars and the deep economic depression of the early 1930s, which emphasized the values of social cohesion over individual interests.

For much of the 20th century, the dominant model of the manager was of someone who gained satisfaction not just from the economic benefits of the job but from the job itself, and from the social status it offered in the interlinked worlds of business, public administration, and the community—the private schooling for the children, the golf club, the charitable associations, and public service committees. The American and European models were much more individualistic than the Japanese one described in the last chapter. There was much more competition for promotion, for example. But there were strong commonalities too. While workers might be paid on piece rates, managers were generally salaried, without any incentive components to their pay. It was commonplace for a manager to build his career in a single firm, and for the firm to take responsibility for his family. Managers were almost all men, and their wives rarely worked (though they were expected to turn out for the company, supporting their husbands on social occasions).

Inside the organization, Western managers had clearer job definitions than their Japanese counterparts, with the emphasis on individual rather than collective responsibility, but this more rigid bureaucracy also afforded comfort and protection. The ambitious could compete up the hierarchy for the top jobs, but the less ambitious could live comfortable lives with a high level of security.

With the increased competition of the 1970s, brought on by steeply rising oil prices, competition from Japan, opening global markets, and new information technologies that allowed new firms to undercut the knowledge-based advantages of more established corporations, these comfortable old bureaucracies began to feel the pressure. In a classic sociological study of an American manufacturing company carried out in the 1940s–1950s, *Men Who Manage*, Melville Dalton had already noted the limitations of formal bureaucracy in dealing with non-routine events in a competitive environment, whether machine breakdowns or urgent customer orders. He found, however, that the managers overcame these limitations by resorting to the less formal setting of the yacht club. Thirty years later in *Moral Mazes*, another classic study of two more manufacturing bureaucracies, now declining in the face of new competition, Robert Jackall found a complete separation between work and the community, and between the moral orders associated with them. Managerial work was dominated by self-interest and a fight for individual survival.

By the early 1980s, bureaucracy had become a synonym for inefficiency. Everyone agreed that organizations, in the public as well as the private sector, needed to be more efficient, more responsive, more flexible, and more innovative. Ways had to be found to release people's natural energy and creativity. One response, discussed in the last chapter, was to use organizational culture to generate social commitments and to energize and direct people's work. Another was to enhance productivity and creativity through individual incentives.

Management and enterprise

From this alternative viewpoint, the problem with bureaucracy (now used as a label for all relatively rigid hierarchical structures) was not that it failed to bind people together in a shared commitment, but that it bound them too tightly, stifling both individual responsibility and individual initiative. The advocates of this view had no core text to compete with the likes of *In Search of Excellence*, but they didn't need one. From the early 1980s onwards, beginning in Ronald Reagan's America and Margaret Thatcher's Britain but quickly spreading across the world, the values of enterprise pervaded the whole of society. Even in the most rigidly bureaucratic of cultures, such as those of Russia and China, individual entrepreneurship flourished, albeit accompanied by that other classic mark of self-interest, corruption. In the developed world, entrepreneurs were lauded, greed became good, and public as well as private sector organizations were rebuilt on the enterprise model.

This movement had deep historical roots, and its emergence in the 1980s had no single cause. Globalization and new technologies played a big part, but so too did secularization and a general build-up of distrust in authority. Its key features can be easily summarized, however.

First there was a growing legitimacy, in all walks of life, of self-interest, and a corresponding weakening of duty. Traditional sources of authority were undermined, and traditional conceptions of moral duty gave way to a range of other moral principles such as self-reliance, fairness, and rights—including the rights of those in possession as well as those of the dispossessed. Second, as traditional moral values were downplayed, money came to be viewed as a measure of everything, and the measurable properties of very short-term effects became prioritized over the much harder to measure long term. Even Japanese firms, at the same time as their long-term focus was being lauded in the West, became markedly more short term.

Third, there emerged a new political orthodoxy of economic egoism and free market capitalism. In a nutshell, it was held that the maximum benefit for society overall (now measured, like everything else, in monetary terms) would be gained by encouraging unconstrained free market competition between actors driven purely by their economic self-interest. The idea, attributed slightly inaccurately to the 18th-century philosopher Adam Smith, was that the price mechanism would ensure the most efficient allocation of resources, and it was applied not only to the liberalization of industrial and financial markets, but also to the managerial labour market.

All this was accompanied, at a more personal level, by a preoccupation with the 'authentic' inner self, and a recasting of social relationships as alliances of like-minded individuals rather than enactments of social bonds that bound differently minded people together. In personal relationships, what mattered was that people were true to themselves, even if in practice this meant being plain selfish. In the context of work, the approved social identity became that of the entrepreneur, conceived in terms of a set of enterprise values: self-motivation, autonomy, personal responsibility, self-regulation, boldness, energy, productivity, efficiency, competitiveness, initiative, innovativeness, creativity, and risk taking.

Some of the strongest advocates of enterprise culture were, rather curiously, traditional moralists, who associated it with a return to 'Victorian values'. In applying the philosophy to a recasting of public sector management, they were also under the strange illusion that people could have all the characteristics of the entrepreneur and still do what they were told and be driven by the goals of the organization. Real entrepreneurs, of course, are driven by their own goals, and are accountable only to themselves. In the public sector, in consequence, which had been characterized for much of the 20th century by a shared commitment to public service, the individualizing move towards enterprise was quickly followed by a massive increase in bureaucratic controls. With the public service ethos fatally undermined and the self-interested entrepreneurial cat let out of the bag, the only way to regain control was through an ever-increasing volume of detailed rules and regulations.

The most striking manifestation of this has been the rise of an audit culture alongside the enterprise culture, with public sector organizations subject to ever more demanding regulatory regimes of self-assessment and external scrutiny. Especially in the health and education sectors (and within these sectors in private as well as public organizations), much of a manager's time is now taken up with the detailed documentation that has to be provided for inspectorates, as well as with the inspections themselves.

These audit regimes are partly an attempt to control managers' new freedoms and partly a means of allocating blame when the attempt fails, and in the latter guise they run through contemporary society. When responsibility becomes individualized rather than shared, people seek to pass it on, and one consequence is that private sector managers are also faced with a heavy burden of externally imposed regulations, especially in areas such as health and safety. If an employee foolishly stands on a chair and falls off, it can no longer be treated as a silly accident. The organization becomes legally liable and the manager slack enough to let such a thing happen becomes accountable. Rather bizarrely, major financial misdemeanours seem to be less troubling, as the large accounting firms responsible for financial audits, themselves embracing the enterprise culture and hungry for fees, have shown themselves repeatedly to be effectively buyable by their clients.

Private sector bosses have generally had fewer illusions than the politicians who directed public sector changes, and as fiercely competitive individuals themselves (a necessary requirement for making it to the top of the business hierarchy) many have been more than happy to play by the new enterprise rules. Managers have been given much more freedom and autonomy, but this has been combined with much higher performance expectations, and much less security of tenure. In an enterprise setting, managers are recognized to be driven primarily by their own individual achievements, measured in terms of salary and promotion, rather than by the achievements of their company, or of the unit they manage. Indeed, high flyers often advance by switching roles—manoeuvring their way out of underperforming or low-profile teams and into more successful ones—and by switching companies, spending little time in any one one place. This is harnessed to the company's aims by individual incentive schemes, from which the top managers themselves have been the greatest beneficiaries. Managers who fail to perform, who in the past would either have been trained up or found a useful niche, are now released: it is, after all, a free market, subject on both sides to the simple laws of supply and demand.

This approach has been taken to its extreme in the financial sector, where performance is most easily measurable. From the

1980s to the 2000s the sector grew massively, and grew massively rich, on the back of it—though arguably at the cost of the real economy, and of society at large. Elsewhere, the values of enterprise have been combined with some of the other features we have reviewed to create a distinctive kind of early 21st-century organization and approach to management, which is sometimes labelled 'post-bureaucracy'.

Management and post-bureaucracy

Contemporary organizations often exhibit a mixture of all the tendencies we have been reviewing. Most large organizations, public or private, are constantly restructuring and re-engineering their processes in a rationalistic search for efficiency. At the same time, they promote a shared commitment to common goals through a strong organizational culture (or what they hope is a strong organizational culture) and a demand on their managers that they treat people in accordance with the positive ideals of the human relations movement. At the same time, they ask people to be entrepreneurial, make extensive use of individual incentives, and hire and fire according to strict market conditions, leaving people 'free' to manage their own careers—or not, as the case may be. Bureaucracies are much more flexible than they used to be, but most organizations still have a clear hierarchical structure. Every manager, apart from the chief executive, has a boss, and every manager is a boss. This is overlaid by personal and informational networks, which provide the main channels of communication. And the core operating elements are semi-autonomous teams, flexibly assembled to meet the challenges of the day.

All of this makes management both more interesting and more demanding. The flexibility, the reduction of management cadres as a result of efficiency drives, and the bureaucratic burdens of accountability all add to the manager's workload and enhance the sense that the task is, literally, endless. And the responsibilities associated with the manager's role all pull in different directions.

Managers have always had multiple responsibilities: to their immediate superiors, to the organization as a whole, to the colleagues or team members with whom they work, to the employees who report to them and rely on their guidance and support, to their families and others who rely on their friendship and care, and of course to their own personal interests. What is striking about post-bureaucracy is that whereas in older and simpler organizational forms these responsibilities were largely aligned, they are now frequently at odds with each other. Self-interest, the interests of other people, and the interests of the company or agency are all in tension. We can see the impact of this by looking at a couple of examples. The core of a manager's job is, arguably, to manage and develop her reports, but this is now in tension with the need to treat them as expendable resources, a corporate need that is reflected in the manager's own incentives and conditions of continuing employment. Again, one of the core challenges of a managerial career is to find a balance between work at home, but this is now, in many organizations, impossible, as meeting the demands of economic security clashes with the demands of family presence and engagement. Partners have long claimed that managers were married to their companies, but there was in the past some social compact, in terms of relative job security. Now there is none.

This is not always the case, by any means. Some companies do provide their managers with socially enriching and secure experiences, while others with a more purely individualistic approach, most obviously in the finance sector but scattered throughout the economy, attract managers who share their values, and whose partners surely recognize that up front. But many organizations are now too conflicted to be anything other than sources of stress.

Theory and practice in contemporary management

Management theory is cumulative. It is developed mainly by social scientists who build, like all scientists, on the findings of their predecessors. Management fashion is cyclical, or at least variable according to circumstances. Wars, for example, tend to bring out the virtues of social bonds and emphasize the dangers of excessive individualism. Economic development provides opportunities for enterprise and highlights the advantages of individualism. Uncertainty prompts a desire for rationalism and rational control mechanisms. Political developments, themselves often responses to social or economic troubles, introduce ways of thinking that are then carried into the management context.

Management practice is influenced by both theory and fashion, and develops both progressively, in response to new levels of scientific understanding, and cyclically, in response to fashion. And of course it varies enormously from company to company, organization to organization. So while the post-bureaucratic management described in the last section may be the dominant contemporary model, it is not the only one. Many organizations are managed in a more rational, more social, or more individual way, and many still rely heavily on traditional or charismatic authority. Many are still managed coercively.

Management practice also depends on the wider cultural context in which the organization is operating. Investment banking and management consulting, for example, tend towards individualism. Heavy engineering tends towards rationalism. The creative industries and—despite decades of enterprise reforms—the public sector exhibit more socializing tendencies.

As we shall see in the next chapter, national cultures also make a big difference to management practices. But before we explore how, we should note explicitly something that will have become increasingly obvious through the last three chapters: the overwhelming dominance of American ideas in management theory. The vast majority of the management theory we have covered originated in America. Even the theory of Japanese management was essentially an American construction. For much of the 20th century it was only really in America that people *studied* management, either as academic researchers or as university students, as opposed to just getting on and doing it. Even in the 1970s and 1980s, management research and teaching were largely restricted to North America, Great Britain, Australia, and New Zealand, and business schools created elsewhere on the American model, often with English as the language of instruction, and with American research literature, American textbooks, and American examples as their stock in trade. Even today, students from the world over go to America and Britain (or American and British schools overseas) for their graduate management training. Hardly anybody travels in the opposite direction.

With management research, management theory, and global management education all built largely on the American model, it is not surprising that the same is often true of management practice. There are, however, some variations, and we shall look at these in the next chapter.

Chapter 7
Management across cultures

Even in America there has been little systematic study of management practice, or of the application of management theories. Outside America there has been hardly any. There have, however, been some large-scale studies of management attitudes across different cultures. The pioneer here was Geert Hofstede, who began conducting attitudinal surveys with IBM executives from around the world in the 1960s and first published an analysis of his findings in 1980. Hofstede identified four, later extended to five, dimensions on which managers' attitudes varied significantly according to their cultural upbringing (see Table 1). From the mid 1980s, Alfons Trompenaars and Charles Hampden-Turner conducted a similar research programme, eventually surveying 34,000 managers from many different companies and countries and analysing their responses to a range of dilemmas framed to capture tensions between complementary values. Beginning in the 1990s, the GLOBE project coordinated by Robert House used local investigators around the world to extend the cultural range of Hofstede's studies, with particular attention to the cultural dimensions of leadership.

Hofstede's analysis has been criticized by other researchers, but his early findings have proved to be fairly robust and were largely supported by the later GLOBE project. Hampden-Turner and Trompenaars aimed for insight rather than academic rigour,

Table 1 Ten countries measured on three of Hofstede's dimensions

To better bring out the comparisons, Hofstede's scales have been rebased and in one case inverted, with the USA set at 100. The two dimensions not covered here are masculinity–femininity, which has been much criticized, and long versus short time horizons, where the surveys were of students rather than managers

Individualism (HIGH) versus Collectivism (LOW)	Uncertainty tolerance (HIGH) versus Uncertainty avoidance (LOW)	Egalitarianism or Low power distance (HIGH) versus Hierarchy or High power distance (LOW)
	Singapore 575	
	China 153	
	UK 131	
	India 115	UK, Germany 114
USA 100	USA 100	USA 100
UK 98		
France 78	Brazil 83	
Germany 74	Germany 71	Japan 74
		S. Korea 67
		France 59
		Brazil 58
India 53	France, S. Korea 54	Singapore 54
Japan 51	Japan 51	India 52
		China 50
Brazil 42		
Singapore, China 22		
S. Korea 20		

83

combining their empirical analysis with observations gleaned from the historical and sociological literatures, and exploring preconceived dimensions of culture rather than trying to extract these dimensions from the data. Their conclusions are, however, consistent with those of the other studies, and more focused on the question of management, and we shall draw on them alongside some of Hofstede's results here. We shall begin by looking at some of the characteristics of American culture, including those that help us to understand why American research teaching has been so dominant in management. We shall then take a snapshot look, inevitably impressionistic, at some of the different attitudes and approaches to be found in other cultural contexts.

Management and American culture

Two of the dimensions explored by Hampden-Turner and Trompenaars were the conceptual dimensions of universalism versus particularism and analysing versus integrating or synthesizing (see Table 2). On both dimensions their surveys showed American culture to occupy an extreme position. In response to a range of dilemmas, American managers came out on average as the most universalistic in their attitudes, believing that the same rules should apply equally and without exception to everybody, regardless of personal or social circumstances. They also came out as the most analytic, reducing problems to their elements rather than viewing them as a whole, and concentrating on the bare facts rather than seeking to contextualize them. Other English-speaking cultures shared the same tendencies, but not to quite the same extent. Japanese, Singaporean, and French managers, by contrast, took much more particularistic and markedly more integrative views, while German managers tended towards universalism but also towards an integrative perspective.

The American combination of universalism and analysis matches the American desire for, and belief in, scientific theories of

Table 2 Typical rankings of six countries on some Hampden-Turner and Trompenaars dimensions

The surveys posed several dilemmas relating to each dimension and the tables below give an impressionistic summary of the comparisons that can be drawn from them rather than single precise measures

Universalism (HIGH) versus Particularism (LOW)	Analysis (HIGH) versus Synthesis (LOW)	Individualist (HIGH) versus Communitarian (LOW)	Inner-directed (HIGH) versus Outer-directed (LOW)	Achieved (HIGH) versus Ascribed (LOW) status
USA	USA	USA	USA	USA
Germany				
UK	UK	Germany	Germany	UK
		UK		
	Germany	France	France	Germany
				France
		Japan	UK	
Japan	Singapore	Singapore	Singapore	Singapore
Singapore	France		Japan	Japan
France	Japan			

management. In simple terms, the combination of universalism and analysis corresponds closely to what I have termed the rationalizing approach, which has dominated American management theory and practice. Scientific management, management by objectives, management science, strategic planning, and process re-engineering all insist on a detailed analytical deconstruction of problems and on universal prescriptions for their solution. Contingency theory uses analysis to bring apparently particularist variations under a single universally applicable theory.

The American approach goes further, however, for even the more particularist and integrative views of management, such as those captured by the human relations movement, McGregor's Theory Y, or the Japanese management principles that became popular in the 1980s, were cast by their American champions as universal theories, derived from empirical analysis. What I have described as the socializing tendency in management becomes, in American research and teaching, as universal and analytic as the tendencies it opposes.

One dimension that was common to all the studies reviewed here was that of individualism versus collectivism or communitarianism (no single word is ideal here, as all carry unwanted connotations). Here again American culture occupies an extreme position. American managers come out as much more individualistic than others, emphasizing individual abilities over interpersonal fit, individual over collective motivation and rewards, individual over group accountability, and individual aims over social expectations. This clearly matches what I have called the individualizing tendency in management, but it can also be seen in the American approach to management education and training. Other cultures tend to see managers as part of the organization and develop them within the organization, through apprenticeships and mentoring. The American approach is to develop individual managers through a business school education, the idea being that they can, as individuals, apply their (universal) knowledge to any organizational setting.

Other characteristics of American management culture suggested by these studies include a relatively low 'power distance,' or high expectation of equal opportunities, and a tendency to link status with achievement rather than position. Hierarchies in American culture are typically based on rational authority, linked to ability and achievement, rather than on traditional authority, and it is current ability that matters. Other cultures—Japan and France, for example—are no less competitive or meritocratic in selecting people to be part of the organizational hierarchy, but once the exams have been passed and the places secured, the hierarchy takes over. Power differentials are accepted and status goes with position. American individualism rebels against this.

American management culture is also at one extreme of the spectrum in its attitude towards time. On Hofstede's measures, Americans have a much shorter-term orientation than respondents from most other cultures. On Hampden-Turner and Trompenaars' measures, American managers have a sequential rather than synchronic approach to time. The past is virtually an irrelevance and the future is distant. Living in the present, they also have a relatively high tolerance of uncertainty. The individualism that separates them from strong social ties, whether at work or in their communities, also works in the time dimension, freeing them from both the bonds of history and concerns as to the future. Universalism, analysis, and their approach to time also combine in a distinct approach to management in which analysis and interpretation are clearly and sequentially separated. American managers may end up 'muddling through' or learning from experience, but they don't normally set out with that intention.

Finally, something that is mentioned only in passing in these studies but has been explored more explicitly in others, American culture more than any other measures things in terms of money. In many ways this acts as a proxy for ability and achievement. In a culture characterized by self-reliance and a strong work ethic, with an orientation towards the present rather than the past, and a suspicion of social ties, inherited wealth has always been treated with ambivalence, but Americans often judge each other by how much they earn. Other cultures are reluctant to reduce complex qualitative values to something so simple. They would distinguish, for example, between monies earned from products or activities of differing value. But in American culture money acts as a perfect universal and analytical measure of individual achievement.

Management in Chinese cultures

At the time much of the research being drawn on here was done, the main interest of American and European management academics was in what could be learnt from Japan. Today, the most natural comparison to make is between American and Chinese management.

Chinese management culture appears to share one feature of the American prototype outlined above. Both Chinese and American managers have a relatively high tolerance of uncertainty. This is linked, however, with quite different perceptions of time. While Americans tend to focus on the very short term, and so do not worry about future uncertainties, the Chinese orientation is so long term that the uncertainties of the present and near future can be dismissed as merely transient.

In other respects too, Chinese and American attitudes appear to be polar opposites. While American culture is highly individualistic, for example, Chinese is highly collectivist, with extremely strong ties to family and, to a lesser extent, community. Social expectations trump personal aims, and social standing trumps, and enables, personal achievements. The Chinese concept of *guanxi* refers to networks of interpersonal relationships within which people pay and repay personal favours and take care of each other's interests. Modelled on familial relationships, these stretch out through extended families and school or community connections to large family-like webs of reciprocal interests and obligations. While Americans believe in equal opportunity for all, and accept authority only when based on ability and achievement, Chinese society and Chinese organizations are much more authoritarian, with large power differentials and hierarchies based on traditional authority, often with an element of coercion.

In contrast to the American tendency to analyse and universalize, Chinese managers adopt an integrative and particularist perspective. Specific circumstances and personal relationships matter more than general rules or principles, and the whole is more important than the parts.

In a society in which family loyalty and *guanxi* are considered far more important than contractual or organizational obligations, it is not surprising that Chinese business tends to be organized on family lines. Even though many large companies are now listed on the stock exchanges, they remain under family control and are typically run as simple hierarchies, with tight control from the top. Many of the older Chinese family companies, based in the capitalist enclaves of Hong Kong, Taiwan, and Singapore, have grown into large multidivisional conglomerates and have long been exposed to Western values and ideas. But while they have adopted Western techniques of marketing, finance, and so on, they are still managed as distinctively Chinese organizations—as, in effect, large multidivisional families, held together more by personal than by contractual relationships.

Japan, South Korea, India

As a general rule, the major Eastern cultures have much more in common with each other than they do with American culture, but each has a distinctive profile. The Japanese management culture, for example, shares much in common with the Chinese, but differs on two crucial dimensions. First, the Japanese have a much lower tolerance of uncertainty than either the Chinese or the Americans. Second, while generally collectivist in their orientation, the Japanese appear to be much more individualistic and materialistic, or money oriented, than other Eastern cultures.

Hampden-Turner and Trompenaars capture the Japanese balance between individualism and collectivism nicely when they say that, while American managers select individuals for a team, Japanese managers make a team from the individuals they are given—and then take collective responsibility for its actions. Similarly, while Americans impose universal rules upon individuals, overriding particular considerations, Japanese derive their rules from the particulars of personal relationships. The Japanese word for 'objectivity,' literally translated, is 'the guest's point of view.' This balance also appears in other respects. Like the Chinese, the Japanese accept high power differentials, and associate authority with status, but the status has first to be earned and the power carries with it responsibilities. Japanese hierarchies may be strong, but they are built on trust and mutual obligations rather than on the top-down imposition of authority. The Japanese perspective is long term, but not as long term as the Chinese, and loyalties and obligations act at the more immediate, medium-term and material level of the organization, rather than at the longer-term and more emotional level of the family.

The collective responsibilities of a family are in some sense idealized in the Japanese organization, which is built around the ideal of harmony (*wa*), whereas in the Chinese context it is the real family, with all its tensions and conflicts, that provides the model. In the Japanese organization trust is built on experience rather than on contract or kinship, and management works through a cyclical process of action and reflection rather than a linear one of analysis and implementation. Consensus and cooperation don't replace competition but complement it. Generally, whereas American managers tend to see things in black and white either/or terms, Japanese managers understand that each side of any opposition contains the seeds of the other and look for both/and resolutions.

South Korea mixes these various elements in yet another way. It shares the strong family culture of China, and its companies are mainly family companies. From the outside the South Korean industrial conglomerates, the *chaibol*, look rather like the Japanese industrial conglomerates or *keiretsu*, but the management of the *chaibol* subsidiaries is traditionally allocated to family members, the authority exerted is much more top down, and there is much less scope for individualism. Korean management practices generally are much closer to the Chinese than to the Japanese model. Korean managers appear much closer to their Japanese counterparts, however, on Hofstede's measures of uncertainty avoidance and timescale orientation, and share much of the Japanese approach to management.

While Chinese and American managers are consistently amongst the most comfortable in the world with uncertainty, Japanese and Korean managers are consistently amongst the least comfortable. They stick rigorously to tight social norms, struggle with change, and seek certainty and security—through hard work, through consensus, and by putting a lot of hard work into achieving consensus. Their time orientation is long term by American standards, and much more synchronic. Past, present, and future are seen as an integrated whole. But it is nothing like so long term as that of Chinese managers. And in Korea, as in Japan, the relatively long-term orientation can be linked to a perception of the company as serving the long-term needs of society, rather than the short-term needs of shareholders.

India offers yet another mix. Like Chinese managers, Indian managers display a very high acceptance of power differences combined with a high uncertainty tolerance. But while their time orientation is relatively long term, it is markedly less so than the other Eastern cultures we have surveyed; and, as in Japan, a general collectivism is moderated by a measure of individualism. Indian management structures are almost always extremely hierarchical, with decisions flowing from the top. Many Indian companies are also family run, and in a socially stratified society who you are counts for more than what you can do. But Indians also love to argue a point. While the Japanese seek consensus and the Chinese brook no argument, Indian management culture allows for argument but ends up with the boss ruling.

Germany, France, Europe, and South America

In general terms, European and South American cultures sit somewhere between the American and Eastern models, with British, Scandinavian, and Dutch managers showing attitudes relatively close to the Americans, and those from Mediterranean and South American cultures showing attitudes similar to those found in the East. Brazil, for example, has a very different history and culture from South Korea, but on the dimensions covered here they seem quite similar. Both have relatively authoritarian attitudes, strong family orientations, relatively long-term perspectives, and a low tolerance for uncertainty. Brazilian culture, as revealed by the managers surveyed, is slightly more individualistic than Korean culture, but it is still relatively collectivist. Spain and Italy are more individualistic still, and much more short term in their orientation, but they are much more authoritarian and collectivist than America or Britain. Their companies tend to be family run and tightly controlled. They are also much more particularist, suspicious of universal rules or theories, and ready to make exceptions; and less analytical, preferring to see a situation as a whole and to trust their intuition.

The two largest European economies, Germany and France, also fit between the extremes, but both are also interesting exceptions. The Germans seem to share something of the Americans' universalism and dislike of power differentials. They believe in universal laws and universal theories, and in ability and achievement. They are more inclined to take a synthetic or holistic than an analytical view, however, and balance individualism against collectivism. German companies, like Japanese ones, have traditionally been conceptualized as working for the long-term benefit of society rather than for short-term profit. They are consensually managed, and they have been slower than other European companies to move towards extreme individual pay incentives for their senior managers. German managers are strong on cooperation and team participation. The Germans also tend to take a synchronic view of time and to adopt a relatively long-term orientation. (Curiously, Hofstede's surveys class them as very short term, but this, the fifth of his dimensions, was based on student rather than manager surveys, and it seems likely that German students who go abroad do so precisely to escape aspects of their own culture. Hampden-Turner and Trompenaars put them at the long-term extreme and this certainly conforms to their attitude to investment—both in companies and as a society—and their strong preference for saving over indebtedness.)

The French, uniquely, manage to be both individualist and showing a high tolerance of power differences. They also have a distinctive view of time. Hampden-Turner and Trompenaars asked their respondents to draw their images of past, present, and future as three circles, and while managers from most cultures tended to draw either the present or the future as the largest circle and the past as the smallest, the French drew theirs the other way round (see Figure 6). History matters in France. Inherited wealth counts for more than current income. French intellectualism is also distinctive, for while the French are great theorizers their theorizing tends to be both holistic and very confined to theory. They do not share the American obsession with empirical facts, and in the practical world take an extreme particularist view. Authority is highly personalized, rules are there to be circumvented by the powerful, and all relationships,

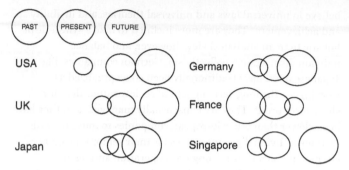

6. Sequential versus synchronic conceptions of time
Hampden-Turner and Trompenaars

whether personal or organizational, are something of a power play. French organizations typically work neither through simple autocracy, like the Chinese, nor through cooperation and consensus, like the Japanese and Germans, but through political negotiation.

Given the space available, the sketches above are inevitably little more than caricatures. Just as in the earlier chapters we described management theories and practices in terms of coexisting tendencies, so the research covered here reveals cultural tendencies, not cultural facts. Hampden-Turner and Trompenaars' questions, in particular, were framed as dilemmas in which both sides had evident value. Within any one culture, different individuals responded to them in different ways, and to describe a culture as universalizing, for example, is simply to say that the respondents exhibited a statistical tendency in favour of a universalizing conception of a situation over a particularizing one. For all their limitations, however, the sketches do give some idea of the range of attitudes to be found in managers from different cultures, and how these can be combined in a variety of ways. Given the American dominance of management theory and education, and the power and reach of American multinationals, management everywhere is nowadays marked by the American

94

model. But even when American management ideas are adopted in other cultures, they are often tailored to the values and needs of the host culture. Personal relationships and traditional forms of authority, in particular, are a much more important part of management practice worldwide than American management dogma would suggest.

Chapter 8
Critical perspectives on management

For those involved in management, whether directly as managers themselves or as consultants or academics, it is mainly a technical and/or a personal affair. For most managers, management is basically a job. The aims and objectives of the job are usually determined by others, and the managers do the job to the best of their ability. They draw on their personal and interpersonal skills, their technical knowledge, and whatever specific management techniques have been adopted by the organization, in ways that vary across cultures, across organizations, and across individuals. Managers might sometimes get tied up in organizational politics, and they might on occasion need to make ethical judgement calls, but these generally appear to be secondary facets of the job. Being a manager is not in itself seen as carrying either political or ethical connotations. Similarly for management consultants and academics, management is just part of the job that they do, a job that in their case is overwhelmingly technical.

Few people become managers, or management consultants, or management academics, out of a sense of vocation. It is not something they do because of a burning desire to express themselves, to contribute to society or to humanity, or to take a stand on issues that matter to them. A successful manager, consultant, or professor might well be proud of her achievements, but being a manager, or working in a management-related area, is rarely in itself a source of great pride. Nor is it something to be ashamed of. It is a job, and a good and respectable job, and for many people an interesting and/or remunerative one, but at the end of the day it's just a job.

For some critics, however, looking at management from the outside, this matter-of-factness appears misleading, even deliberately so. From a critical perspective, management can seem deeply political and far from value free. For many blue-collar workers and those on the political left, managers have always been representatives of financial capital and agents of exploitation. For many financial investors, arguably the true representatives and manipulators of capital, business managers have long been cast as thieves, using shareholder capital to run businesses in their own selfish interests rather than in the 'proper' (but equally selfish) interests of shareholders. More recently, professionals in education and health services and the arts have seen managers as their ideological opponents, imposing 'managerial' values (efficiency, the profit motive) on cultural and public service institutions in which they have no place. And for 'critical management' scholars, in the world of academia, the practice of management is deeply implicated in the exercise of power and privilege.

Between capital and labour

When the term 'management' is used as a collective noun to describe the managers within an organization, it almost always carries connotations of conflict. For employees who are not themselves managers, management are typically 'them'; they are not part of 'us' and they are implicitly or explicitly conceived as hostile to 'us.' Managers themselves may not feel this division so strongly, but they are constantly reminded of it, especially in times of industrial strife, and they too distinguish a 'we', responsible for managing the organization (note the use of the nominative case—the we who act rather than the us who are acted upon), from a 'them', who have to be managed.

In theoretical terms, this conflict is normally characterized as a conflict between labour and capital. The theory derives from the writing of Karl Marx. Writing in *Capital* (1867), Marx identified productivity gains in industry both from the division of labour (as had been noted earlier by Adam Smith) and from the combination of workers with the same skills, as was by then commonplace in the large textile factories of Britain. Man, he observed, was a social animal, who could gain from cooperation, and the economies of scale associated with the factory system (in which many identical machines might be housed in one building and driven from one power source) favoured ever-growing firms. The capitalist owners of these firms paid the workers what was necessary to keep them working—essentially just what they would be able to earn on their own, without the productivity gains of the firm—and appropriated the surpluses derived from the productivity gains to themselves. In purely economic terms this was an effective engine of growth, as the surpluses generated could be reinvested in further labour and machinery to generate further surpluses. But in political terms this growth was the product of class conflict, achieved through the exploitation and oppression of the workers by the monied upper classes.

The role of managers in this Marxist account has always been ambiguous. Even the factories of Marx's time required some kind of intermediaries between the owner and the workforce, but as we noted in Chapter 3 these early managers were drawn from both the owner's family and the workforce. The latter group, responsible for supervision and discipline, were both employees and agents of capital. Then, when the new class of professional managers came on the scene around the turn of the century, they were most naturally associated neither with the capitalist class of the monied owners nor with the working class of the labourers but with the growing middle class of educated professionals and self-made businessmen.

From the perspective of the workers, and for most Marxist analysts, managers as a class have primarily been seen, despite their employee status, as agents of capital. Scientific management and its rationalizing successors were easily categorized as systems of oppression by which managers wrested control of the production process from the workers, and in the process maximized the value that could be appropriated from them for the owners' use. And while this may not have been the intention of these systems' advocates, it is pretty much how things worked out in practice—and how they often still do, in many industrial and retail contexts. Consider, for example, the way counter staff at McDonald's work to tightly scripted routines, their jobs reduced to acting as they are told, and their wages reduced accordingly.

Meanwhile, however, in the course of the 20th century, managers also came under criticism for *not* acting in the interests of capital. In the 1930s Adolph Berle and Gardiner Means identified a 'separation of ownership and control' in American corporations, as a diversification of ownership through the public sale of stocks and shares combined with a shift of management control from family owner-managers to employed professionals.

This raised two sets of problems. One was social. The family firms of the 19th century had invested heavily in their local town communities, to which they were closely bound. The profits went to the family, who lived in the community and relied on it for their workers: it was natural to invest in schools, charities, etc. In 20th-century corporations, however, a local factory would be managed by an employee. The firm's profits were not his to spend and the link with the community was broken. The other problem was, in a sense, the other side of the same coin. Since the managers of a corporation were no longer its owners, there was a conflict of interest between their brief to maximize profits for the owners and the temptation to serve their own interests: by expanding the firm so as to create more or better management jobs, for example, by indulging the labour force to create a more comfortable environment, or by taking steps to prevent takeovers.

The first of these problems was hotly debated at the time, but very quickly forgotten. The second was initially set aside as practically insolvable, but re-emerged with the advent of economic agency theory in the 1970s and has dominated debates on corporate governance ever since. In a review of corporate governance research, economists Andrei Shleifer and Robert Vishny described the core problem as being 'how investors get the managers [assumed here to be completely self-interested] to give them back their money.'

Financially, the most senior managers have done pretty well out of this obsession. The incentive pay packages designed to tie their interests to those of the shareholders have left them far richer than their predecessors. And whatever their initial sympathies, many have no doubt been co-opted to the interests of financial capital. Middle and junior managers, however, have done less well, and arguably find themselves exploited in much the same way as blue-collar workers have been in the past. As every ounce of performance is squeezed out of them, the value created is appropriated by others, and with regular redundancies and competitive job markets, both the financial rewards and the quality of life traditionally associated with management have been eroded.

Any business manager has both a responsibility to the owners or shareholders of a company for maximizing its profits and a duty of care in respect of its employees. Managers are almost inevitably stuck in the middle between capital and labour, and between the class interests associated with these. In the post-war heyday of management, which was also, and not coincidentally, the heyday of middle-class values and middle-class dominance of the political agenda, these responsibilities came with a high social status. Managers were the pillars of their local communities, respected for their integrity and for their responsibility, and generally able to take the higher ground in any political encounter. In a few countries, most notably Germany, this is still largely the case. In the last twenty years, however, a new financial class has emerged, securing a massive proportion of the wealth of both developed and developing economies and with it a dominant political position. From holding the dominant centre ground, management is now in danger of becoming the squeezed middle, despised and exploited by capital for its lack of enterprise and by labour for its lack of solidarity.

Management and professional values

This ambiguity in management's position is reflected in discussions of managerial values, both in practice and in the academic literature. Since the work of managers is primarily concerned with the management of people, we might imagine that managerial values would reflect the things that matter most to people: human feelings, moral virtues, and so on. The dominance of the rationalizing tendency in management has, however, tended to exclude such things. Indeed, for the philosopher Alasdair McIntyre, writing around 1980, this was precisely what distinguished the archetypal character of the manager:

> Managers themselves and most writers about management conceive of themselves as morally neutral characters whose skills enable them to devise the most efficient means of achieving whatever end is proposed. Whether a given manager is effective or not is on the dominant view a quite different question from that of the morality of the ends which his effectiveness serves or fails to serve.

On this view, which does indeed dominate the business schools and management consulting, and which can also be found in many areas of management practice, management is a purely technical affair. It has nothing to do with human values as commonly conceived, but operates entirely within the value structure of economic rationality and efficiency. This is what raises the hackles of teachers and nurses, who believe passionately that their schools, universities, and hospitals should be dedicated to people, not profit, and who cast their managers as traitors and turncoats. As with the relationship between management and capital, however, what is unclear is the extent to which this approach is chosen by managers and the extent to which it is imposed upon them.

One of the most penetrating analyses of the managerial condition is that conducted by sociologist Stanley Deetz in *Democracy in an Age of Corporate Colonization*—a book whose title gives little clue to its contents. According to Deetz, the modern corporation (and, we might add, the large organization more generally) is characterized by a way of thinking and behaving that he labels as managerialism and that has quite distinctive features. The most striking of these is an emphasis on means over ends, to the point at which the means become the ends. Economic efficiency takes centre stage, and all questions of purpose or values are not just neglected but actively suppressed. Moral issues, for example, cannot be openly discussed at work, and can only be resolved when converted into economic terms—when reduced, in effect, to questions of pricing. Emotional concerns, too, are out of court and, since any individual problems always raise the possibility of an intrusion of values or personal concerns, decision making is routinized as much as possible.

This picture clearly has a large element of truth. Managers, and employees generally, for example, will often speak to their loved ones at home of moral issues that worry them at work, yet feel quite unable to raise those issues within the work organization. Managerialism in this sense also clearly serves some collective or class interests of managers. The world of rational analysis and economic efficiency is the world in which they—and the teachers and consultants who live off them—are expert. The exclusion of questions of purpose, moral value, and emotional experience effectively marginalizes not only the workers, their families and communities, and other stakeholders who might be affected by the corporation, but also any owners whose interests in the firm might conflict with the instrumental interests of management. Even when the owners are themselves interested primarily in profit, the managers' claim to expertise secures for them the freedom to make any business decisions.

At the same time, however, managers are as much victims of this managerialism as they are beneficiaries from it. It is their scope for personal or moral judgement that is circumscribed, and while some might welcome this—a purely technical job can be a welcome escape from the demands of family life—many do not. As Deetz noted, managerialism also carries with it the seeds of its own demise. The more routine and technical management work becomes, the less apparent need there is, especially in a world of sophisticated information systems and decision tools, for managers. The rise of technical management was often described in terms of professionalization, but a key feature of the professions is that they are characterized by the exercise of judgement, including moral judgement, as well as by a base of scientific and technical training. The early business schools recognized this and treated management techniques as tools to be judiciously employed, but in recent decades the techniques have taken over and management has arguably become less of a profession, more of a trade.

Critical management studies

The vast majority of academic work in management is functional in orientation. Its aim is to improve management techniques and build a basis of knowledge in the applied social sciences that will help people to manage more effectively—which generally means more efficiently. Deetz's book, published in 1992, was one of the seminal works in a very different tradition of scholarship. This has sought to understand management and organizations in a way that is descriptive rather than prescriptive. It has sought in particular to describe some of the social and political forces underlying the dominant practices and discourses of management: to critically question and unpick the taken-for-granted assumptions underlying mainstream management thought and practice. Deetz himself drew on the work of two other pioneers in this field, Mats Alvesson and Hugh Willmott, whose book *Making Sense of Management: A Critical Introduction* became its core text. Building on these foundations, there is now a sizeable body of research going under the name of 'critical management studies'.

The word 'critical' here referred initially to a tradition of Marxist critique and to the Marxist-influenced 'critical theory' of a particular school of sociology known as the Frankfurt School. Critical management studies today encompass a wide range of theoretical perspectives, drawn from both social theory and psychoanalysis, but the dominant influences, in Deetz's work and since, are those of Marxist critique, the critical theory of Jürgen Habermas (from the Frankfurt School) and the poststructuralism of the French social theorist Michel Foucault. From Marxist critique and critical theory, critical management studies inherit a concern with how systems of exploitation are disguised so as to appear legitimate and operate with the consent of those exploited. What appear on the face of it to be natural, necessary, and self-evident features of a social order are social and political constructions, which naturalize and universalize particular class interests.

A particular focus is on Habermas's distinction (drawn from Weber) between instrumental means-oriented rationality and practical ends-oriented rationality. In the modern corporation, as in modern society more generally, it is argued, means-oriented reasoning lays claim to the whole space of reason, excluding morality, judgement, and the give and take of reasonable dialogue. In management, even the human factors of dialogue and consensus and the socializing tendencies discussed in Chapter 5 become mere means to rational control, and to the extension of that control to cover employees' feelings as well as their actions.

More generally, critical management scholars have pointed to the ways in which seemingly objective criteria such as those of rationality and efficiency are to some extent socially and politically determined. What counts as rationality, for example, can be contested. Weberian rational authority privileges particular interests just as much as the traditional authority it has replaced. Rationalizing approaches to management privilege the interests of an educated class over those of an experienced workforce and, historically at least, those of men over women. Notions of efficiency and economic rationality privilege those whose interests are financial and short term over those whose interests are long term and hard to calculate.

The second stream of critical management studies comes from Foucault and in particular from his conception of power–knowledge relations. For Foucault, the social world is the product of numerous competing and interacting discourses: systems of thought and expression (physical as well as linguistic) that shape our views of ourselves and the world around us. The product of ever-changing forces, these views are fragmented and unstable, and the same applies to power relationships. Whereas critical theorists see the established order as the product of dominant political interests, Foucauldians see power as inherent in the discursive structures themselves, in the words and expressions we choose, the forms of knowledge we admit, the ways we conceive of relationships, and the routines we adopt to order and make sense of our lives.

These routines can be imposed, and a particular form of power arises when disciplinary practices replace overtly coercive relationships—when workers become ruled by the production line, for example, or managers by the principles of financialization, by audit cultures, or by specific management techniques. But in Foucault's world there is always scope for resistance, all relationships are situationally specific, and it makes little sense to talk of the holder or of the exercise of power. From this perspective the rationalizing ideology of management is neither something that is imposed by one group on another nor something that is objectively right and appropriate, but something that has arisen from particular social-historical circumstances and is at the same time both a resource and a constraint on managerial action.

Critical management scholars have tended to focus more on uncovering oppression than on remedying it. Indeed, there is a curious division of labour in academic management studies, as mainstream scholars, focused on improving management techniques, are reluctant to step back and view management as a phenomenon to be understood, while critical management scholars have been equally reluctant either to step outside their particular theoretical base and seek an understanding of management more broadly or to engage with managers and put their findings to productive use. Habermas's own primary concern was emancipatory: to recover a wider conception of reasoning than has come to dominate contemporary life and give voice, through open dialogue, to those whose interests have been overridden. Foucault too was concerned to empower minorities and open up the political space. Applied to management, however, such aims are still largely a project for the future.

Chapter 9
Management
as sense-making

One of my aims in this book has been to make sense of management for readers who may have little knowledge or experience of it. The way we make sense of things is by fitting them into a narrative or story. Here I have mainly told a story of the generation of management theory and the development of management practice, in which managers and management scholars take centre stage. I have also told something of two other stories: one in which managers are the villains rather than the heroes, and one in which they are mere bit-part players, taking roles shaped for them by social, cultural, and economic forces beyond their control. Many teachers and academics insist on sticking to just one of these stories. In much the same way, politicians insist upon a particular story about the state of the country and the problems it faces. But the world is rarely that simple. Each story highlights something important, but at the cost of hiding or denying something equally important. Whatever our preferred way of making sense of things, there is always another way in which we could have made sense of them.

As well as being characters in other people's stories, managers are also storytellers themselves. As we saw in Chapter 2, an important part of what managers do is make sense of their environments, both for themselves and especially for the people working in the units they manage. Sometimes this entails little more than passing on, or suitably adapting, the stories they have been told by their bosses: this is where the organization has come from, this is where it's going, why, and how. But sometimes, and especially when acting as leaders, managers also need to be their own sense-makers.

The importance of sense-making

Organization scholars use the term 'sense-making' in a specific and quite complex way. Karl Weick, in his definitive survey, takes sixty pages to define it and another hundred to refine that definition. Very roughly, though, it refers to the ongoing process by which we individually and collectively rewrite what has happened in the past to make sense of the the present, fitting past and present together in plausible stories, based round acceptable versions (acceptable, that is, both to ourselves and to others) of the kind of people we are.

We noted earlier Herbert Simon's observation that we can never hope to fully analyse the world around us, or indeed get anywhere near such an analysis, and so satisfice or settle for a 'good-enough' analysis. The idea of sense-making starts from the observation that the world is even more complex than that suggests. Both the social and the psychological worlds in which we live are so complex and so rich as to be effectively malleable and open to a wide range of interpretations. As soon as we get beyond the simplest of facts or events, extracting an objective view, or getting the facts straight, is well-nigh impossible. We have to have some version of events, however, some frame of reference within which to act, or we would be completely impotent. And we need a version of events that enables us to live with ourselves—that confers an identity that is both stable and acceptable. Collectively, we also need a version of events that allows us to make sense of each other's words and actions and so interact socially. These stories need a certain factual consistency, but since we never have a perfect knowledge of the facts, plausibility is more important than accuracy.

An important characteristic of sense-making is that it is retrospective. At a simple level we can only pay attention to something once it has happened, and we can't really understand even what we're doing ourselves until after we've done it. Even if we have a prior reason for doing something, when we look back on it we can always question that reason or find other reasons. Actions also commit us to certain stories, as we retrospectively justify them and make them intelligible to ourselves and others. The sociologist Harold Garfinkel observed that trial juries do not agree on what facts are important and then reach a verdict, but reach a verdict first and then agree on which facts are important.

Juries are faced with a particular situation as they are typically forced to choose between two more or less plausible stories, both of which somehow fit the facts. They have little option but to choose a story and fit the facts to it. But their situation is not so different from that of everyday life. Each of us has developed a story of the world and of our place in it with which we are reasonably comfortable. Most of the time we fit new events, new experiences, and new social interactions into that story, perhaps modifying it in minor ways, but without seriously questioning it. Sometimes an event occurs that is so dissonant with our sense of things that we have to reconsider and make sense anew. But we don't normally do this by going back to the facts and analysing them afresh. Rather we look for alternative stories that might give a better and more comfortable fit, and to which the known facts can be accommodated.

Another characteristic of sense-making is its dependence on cultural assumptions and beliefs. We saw in the last chapter how some critical management scholars see management, management practices, and management knowledge as ideological constructs. This is in itself a way of making sense of things that throws light on some aspects while inevitably hiding others. But the recognition that any sense-making goes beyond mere facts and relies as well on ideology, culture, emotion, and so on is not the sole preserve of critics. Facts only become meaningful when held together by theories, and in trying to make meaningful sense of everyday life the connecting theories we draw on—the only ones we can draw on—are those provided by our beliefs, values, and feelings.

Finally, sense-making is not just a reflective process but an active one. In acting according to our sense of the world, we not only commit ourselves to that sense but also impose it on others. Our words and actions carry expectations of responses, and it is the pattern of action and response, expectation and confirmation, that maintains the stability of the socially constructed world in which we live.

Sense-making in organizations

Sense-making takes place in all aspects of life, but it is especially apparent in organizations. In everyday social life we are not continuously called on to give sense-making accounts. Our lives are dominated by relationships of kinship and friendship that develop relatively slowly, and in which meaning is collectively shared and rarely challenged. Only when something quite dramatic happens, socially, politically, or emotionally, does sense-making come to the foreground. Organizations are more fluid communities. People come and go, and the newcomers, generally complete strangers, have to be instantly accommodated. This means that the collective stories that hold organizations together have to be more explicit, and more explicitly constructed, than those of families or communities. And just as organizations are more artificial than other social groupings, so their stories are more obviously artifices.

Organizational environments tend to impinge more directly, through competitive pressures, for example, or financial results, and to change more rapidly. This puts pressures on sense-making because on the one hand there is a greater pressure for the stories to change and adapt to new circumstances, while on the other hand the fact that the stories are more explicit makes them much harder to change. In everyday life we tend to slide gradually from one story to another, first quietly omitting elements that no longer fit, then gradually introducing new elements that do. That depends, however, on being able to temporarily fudge or avoid things, which is much harder with the more explicit stories of organizations.

At the individual level, people are both more accountable and more vulnerable as employees in an organization than they are as members of a community. Impacted by promotions or non-promotions, performance measures, and the threat of redundancy, personal identities are much more fragile. And whereas in private life you can keep yourself to yourself and keep quiet while your sense of things develops, a manager has no such freedom. She always has to be prepared to give an account of herself to others—an account that makes sense in terms of a wider story.

As well as imposing a requirement to speak, organizations also impose a particular requirement to act. In social life, when things change, we can often take time to make sense of the change. We can be inactive for a while, sitting on the fence, not committing ourselves in either words or actions until we have developed a story with which we are comfortable. People in work organizations, however, are not paid to be inactive. They are paid, and managers in particular are paid, to act. They are also paid to keep up with fast-changing environments. Especially in a competitive environment, a good understanding of yesterday's problems is unlikely to impress. What is called for is an understanding of today's problems, however imperfect that might be. In an organizational setting, sense-making is consequently more likely to proceed from action. You act and then, having acted, construct a story to justify the action and make sense of it for those around you.

Managers as sense-makers

The sense-making perspective gives us interesting insights to several aspects of management. Here we shall look very briefly at three of them: decision making, leadership, and the management of change.

A common perception of managerial work is that managers solve problems and make decisions or choices. Before solving a problem, however, you first have to formulate it, and that is arguably the real management challenge. It is only by making sense of a situation that a manager can formulate a problem in a way that is meaningful, and once a problem is formulated in a particular way the solution tends to fall out. By the time you reach the point of making a decision, the decision has effectively been made. If we take a simple example, in which a manager chooses between investing in one product or another, this may look, when she presents it, like a simple calculation. But what matters is what she chooses to measure: what criteria are important, how they are weighted, and so on. And that in turn depends on the way the company makes sense of the world (its strategy and values) and the particular sense she makes when applying that company story to the situation she faces.

To take another example, a change in the environment may often be depicted either as a threat or as an opportunity. Depending on how it is presented, how it is made sense of, people will likely respond quite differently, even if the data they are faced with are just the same. A manager asked to respond to a threat will reach different decisions from one asked to respond to an opportunity.

Decisions don't always fall out in this way. Sometimes managers need to take decisions, to act decisively, without any story to guide them. In this case the action effectively writes the story—as when faced with two life paths and no clear rationale for deciding between them we commit ourselves one way or the other and in doing so 'decide' on who we are. In a management situation, however, where the decision is not just personal, such an action needs a story behind it. Weick recounts a tale, first told by the physiologist Albert Szent-Gyorti, of a detachment of soldiers lost in an unexpected and prolonged snow storm in the Alps. After three days they had been given up for lost, but they returned safely after one of them found a map in his pocket which they used to get their bearings and find their way home. When their captain asked to see it, though, he saw that it was a map of the Pyrenees, not the Alps. The idea here is that it didn't matter that it was the wrong map. It was a map, and a plausible map, and it enabled the men to act rather than giving up in despair.

To illustrate what happens when there is no map, Weick offers an interpretation of some famous experiments conducted by Stanley Milgram in the 1950s. Here volunteers were asked to take part in a 'learning' experiment in which subjects were given increasingly severe electric shocks, administered by the volunteers, if they failed to give correct responses to the investigator. In fact the experiments were faked and the subjects receiving the shocks were not more volunteers, as those administering the shocks were told, but actors. What Milgram found was that when calmly instructed by the investigator, volunteers were prepared to increase the shocks delivered to lethal levels, despite clear evidence of the suffering of the subjects. This is generally taken as an illustration of unquestioning obedience in the presence of authority, but it can also be seen as an illustration of what happens when people have no way of making sense of a situation. With no sense-making story on which to rely, they lose their ability to act and simply do as they are told.

Organizations need people to take action, and if people are to take action they need sense-making frameworks. You can give someone all sorts of information but unless you also give them a story or framework to make sense of it, they will be stymied. An important part of a manager's job is to make sure people have such a framework, and sometimes, when none is available, she may have to make it up. That is when management becomes leadership. Just as we are often told that any decision is better than no decision, so any map or framework is better than no map or framework, and a major part of leadership is sense-giving.

As we noted in Chapter 2, management as leadership is particularly important in times of change, and in times of change organizational sense-making becomes especially challenging. We noted above that organizational stories are particularly hard to adapt. Once a particular 'sense' of things becomes established and shared there is always a tendency, in any context, for any new evidence or new events to be interpreted according to the established story. This tendency is exacerbated in organizations by the explicit nature of the story and the frequency with which it needs to be retold. It is also exacerbated by the effects of 'groupthink', which we introduced in Chapter 4. In business organizations, where the ways in which things are understood are typically ways that have been competitively successful in the past, the competitive environment can be both an impetus for change and at the same time a constraint on change taking place. New events that might signal to an outsider the need for change are either ignored or interpreted, and if necessary reinterpreted, as confirming the existing view of things—or at most some modest adjustment to that view. It takes a major shock, a severe dissonance, to force a change of view.

Organizations need to change to adapt to their changing environments, but this is a real challenge for managers. In businesses the chief executive is often a leading author of the prevailing view of things and personally identified with the current strategy. The senior managers have all bought in to a shared sense of things. So much is invested in continually repeating a consistent story—for employees and, in larger companies, for shareholders and the press—that challenging this story is almost impossible. Similarly at middle management level, the need to make sense of things in terms of the approved corporate story limits the ability to make new sense of them in response to outside influences. The need to educate new staff into the thinking of the organization limits the ability to make productive use of their fresh, outsiders' eyes.

Large companies eventually change their stories when their financial results become unsustainable or press comment becomes unbearable. They then typically change their chief executives and look to newcomers, who have the benefit of a few months' grace to sort out their sense-making, to provide new stories. If sold aggressively enough down the line, these may replace the old ones. This process is difficult enough, but it relies heavily on external factors to undermine the established ways of looking at things. When organizations are less exposed to external critiques or market forces, change is even harder. Here managers have not only to create new stories, but also to find effective ways of challenging the old ones, or else modifying and reinterpreting them, artificially recreating, on accelerated timescales, the processes that occur naturally in everyday life.

Chapter 10
Management and morality

From Chapter 8, we have a picture of management as amoral and of modern organizations as settings from which all questions of morality are excluded. The strong individualizing tendencies of contemporary management, described in Chapter 6, point in the same direction. For critics of management the absence of moral considerations is a fault, but for the advocates of contemporary approaches to management it is both an empirical fact of life and an economic virtue. On this view of the world, this way of making sense of things, people are naturally self-interested and the way in which societies most effectively generate wealth is by not interfering with that self-interest. If managers were to worry about morals this would simply make their organizations less efficient.

From Chapter 2, on the other hand, we have a picture of management practice as an inherently social activity that would seem to have an essential moral dimension. This picture is reinforced by our discussion of the socializing tendencies in management in Chapter 5 and by the metaphor with which we began the book, in which the work of a manager was likened to the 'coping' or 'managing' of a harassed parent under domestic pressures. And if managers are indeed authors and storytellers, as suggested in Chapter 9, that too would seem to imply some moral responsibilities. Returning to the domestic analogy, the stories we tell to our children as we make sense of the world for them are the foundations of their moral education. It would be strange if the stories told by managers were entirely free of ethical or moral content.

While this tension takes different forms in different cultural and organization settings, it has long been endemic to management. The traditional bureaucratic corporation was in many ways a traditional moral community, modelled on the societies in which it operated. Hierarchical structure was accompanied by an ethic of duty, in which each member served the interests of the whole by conscientiously playing his or her particular part. Critics argue that this was morally disabling. The bureaucracy established rules for everything and the manager, acting as an office holder rather than as an individual person, could not do other than follow those rules, even if the purposes of the organization were quite unethical. Sociologist Zygmunt Bauman pointed to the bureaucratic organization that made possible the Holocaust as an example of the dehumanizing effects of bureaucratic technology.

While there was always a risk that a bureaucracy could be turned to immoral ends by unscrupulous leaders, however, that was essentially a pathological state. It relied on the exercise of power, through charisma and coercion, in ways that were completely alien to the bureaucratic ideal. In a properly functioning bureaucracy the leader or chief executive is as much a servant of the community as anyone else. The duty of the employee to the organization is accompanied by a reciprocal duty on those in charge, to look after employees and respect their private lives. And both the impartiality expected of the managers and the rules they are expected to follow have a moral basis. Rather than excluding morality, it could be said that the bureaucracy imposes a particularly strict form of morality, in which moral duties allow of no exceptions.

Other forms of hierarchy achieve similar effects in ways appropriate to their own cultures. The hierarchies of Chinese companies, for example, are far more personal, relying as much on traditional as on rational authority. The morality they impose is one of personal and familial loyalty, and this reflects the dominant morality of Chinese society. Japanese companies impose a morality of consensus that appears less authoritarian. In recognizing everybody's viewpoint, and in accepting the long-term obligations that follow from employment, they look more like ideal moral communities. But the morality still serves to silence critics: the consensus, once reached, is binding. And while the Japanese corporation may protect the narrow interests of the managers, it cares little for their families.

Even post-bureaucratic organizations, with their much lesser reliance on hierarchy, impose a kind of morality. But in this case the tension is sharper as the morality imposed is one of self-interest. Of course, you cannot impose self-interest in the same way as you can impose obedience to rules or bosses. The manager in post-bureaucracy is still free to act as a traditionally moral agent, taking care of the interests of others. But she is also 'free' to lose her job if she doesn't perform to the expected standards. Moreover, such is the relentless pressure to perform that it can be difficult to find the space for moral reflection. If we look at the most prominent failures of business ethics in recent years—the behaviours that brought down Enron and Arthur Andersen, for example, or WorldCom or Lehman Brothers—it is clear that many people knew or felt that something wrong was going on. They were just too preoccupied with financial performance, their own and their company's, to stop and think about it.

Within the financial sector, which is where these and many other recent ethical scandals occurred, the values of financial self-interest are aggressively promoted. Companies in this sector often seem to operate in a world of their own in which everything is treated like a high-stakes computer game, completely disconnected from the ordinary world of people and things, and in which normal moral concerns really are seen as irrelevant. Like computer games themselves, moreover, financial trading is compulsive and all-consuming, leaving people with neither the time nor the energy to reflect on anything beyond the immediate demands of the job. In companies in other sectors, and in other kinds of organization, which interact more directly with everyday life, both the bias towards self-interest and the pressures of work are probably less extreme.

In this more general context it can be argued that much of the technical side of management can now be done using computerized systems, and that what is left for human managers is precisely the task of moral leadership. The central functions of managers, on this view, are to generate a common interest out of people's individual interests, to provide stories that can engage people's full potentials, and not just their technical skills, and to use their judgement to deal with the exceptions arising from particular personal circumstances.

Let us go back to the practice of management and to the kinds of situation with which managers are faced on a day-to-day basis. For example, a high-flying employee finds herself, through no fault of her own, needing to adapt her work hours to make time for her small child. She's prepared to put in the fifty-plus hours a week of the rest of her team, but she needs a few hours a day of protected time, away from emails, texts, and telephone calls. Her team colleagues are initially sympathetic but after a few weeks get impatient and angry. The time she needs at home is precisely the time when they find it most convenient to meet, and the manager has to sort things out. Or take another example. A manager is trying to put together a team for an important assignment and has to choose between an experienced employee who will perform satisfactorily or a younger one who may do brilliantly, may do badly, but is ready to be tested and needs the learning experience.

There are no technical answers to this kind of dilemma. A manager has to judge the situation based on the specific circumstances, the individuals involved, the dynamics of the work group, and so on. And how the decision is implemented—the story told, the sense made—is just as important as the choice made. Moreover, a big part of that story is moral. If a manager is to be effective, her choices have to be seen to be fair, to be respectful and caring of the people affected, to be dutiful in respect of the organization, and so on.

When we come back to the everyday practice of management, we come back to a situation not unlike that of managing domestic crises. The family situation is different in various ways. Feelings and emotions are more to the fore and expressing them is more acceptable, even expected. The social norms governing everyday life (the behaviours other people expect of us) are different from those governing life at work. We are far more aware in a domestic context that while acting in our short-term interest may have its attractions—and may even, these days, be socially acceptable—it won't necessarily make us happy in the long term. We cannot change families or even communities as easily as we can change jobs, and this affects both our own behaviour and our expectations of how others may behave. But managers are still people, and though the stories they tell about themselves might differ in some respects, they are basically the same people in the office as they are at home. They still have feelings, and they are still capable of responding to the feelings of others and of making reasonable practical judgements. The time pressures of managerial work may be demanding, but those of family life are not exactly undemanding, especially for working mothers, those with responsibilities for disabled relatives, or those who take on heavy responsibilities in their communities.

In both cases, ethical behaviour rests on a determination to engage with ethical issues. If people are only interested in themselves, whether actively harming others to get their own way or just neglecting others in favour of their own comfort, they will not make good managers or good parents, whether under pressure or not.

Moreover, while the ethical situations that arise in a management context are often peculiar to that context, they don't pose particular technical difficulties. There are issues in the ethics of science and medicine where the development of new technologies (genetic engineering would be an example, or the technologies to keep people alive when they would otherwise die) poses questions that haven't arisen before, and that bring with them deep philosophical challenges. But the situations faced by managers are rarely like that. They may require some technical knowledge of the context—of accounting methods or marketing or engineering and so on—but faced with an issue that is clearly ethical, most managers can tell right from wrong quite as easily as they can in everyday life. The challenge is not so much in resolving the issue once it is acknowledged as in facing up to it in the first place.

This is why the pressures of managerial work are so important. Relatively few managers are outright unethical (though a few, it has to be said, are, and they can do enormous damage). Most managers, like most people generally, are well intentioned. But most managers, again like most people, are also weak, in that faced with a difficult situation they will tend to look for an easy way out. The pressures of managerial work make it hard to find time and brain space for moral reflection, but they also make it easy *not* to find that time and space, easy to put difficult issues aside. The stronger those pressures, the stronger the manager has to be to overcome them, but this is more a question of willpower than of time and energy. And while there are situations in which ethical behaviour would require the strength of a saint, in most cases it requires no more than a normal moral awareness and the discipline to make a little time in the day for reflection (a few minutes may be enough); to listen to what people mean as well as what they say; and to be alert and attentive to their needs. All this can be hard to do, and harder still to sustain, but it is not impossibly hard, and at the end of the day it is what makes management—rather like bringing up a family—so rewarding and worthwhile.

References and further reading

Chapter 1: Management and managing

The observations that management is about coping as much as
control, and that the challenges of managerial work are very
similar to those of managing a family, are no doubt commonplace, but they are especially characteristic of Charles Handy.
See for example:

Handy, Charles, 1978/2009, *Gods of Management: The Changing
World of Organizations*. Souvenir Press.

The other key source for the view presented here is the work
of Herbert Simon. See in particular his classic work, originally
published in the 1940s:

Simon, Herbert A., 1997, *Administrative Behaviour: A Study of
Decision Making Processes in Administrative Organizations*. 4th
edition. Free Press.

I have discussed the assumptions underlying economic agency
theory and their possible alternatives in:

Hendry, John, 2002, 'The principal's other problems: honest
incompetence and management contracts', *Academy of
Management Review*, 27(1): 98–113.

Chapter 2: The work of the manager

The best recent survey of managerial work, and the one on which
this chapter draws most heavily, is:

Mintzberg, Henry, 2009, *Managing*. FT Prentice Hall.

A valuable collection of papers on and around the subject is:

Tengblad, Stefan, 2012, *The Work of Managers: Towards a Practice Theory of Management*. Oxford University Press.

The major studies that best capture the quality of managerial work are those of new managers, especially:

Hill, Linda A., 2003, *Becoming a Manager: How New Managers Master the Challenges of Leadership*. Harvard Business School Press.

Watson, Tony and Harris, Pauline, 1997, *The Emergent Manager*. Sage.

Other classic studies that are still well worth reading include:

Sayles, Len R., 1979, *Leadership: What Effective Managers Really Do... and How They Really Do It*. McGraw-Hill.

Stewart, Rosemary, 1982, *Choices for the Manager*. Prentice Hall.

Kotter, John P., 1982, *The General Managers*. Free Press. For highlights see Kotter, 1982, 'What effective managers really do', *Harvard Business Review*, 60(6): 156–62.

Watson, Tony, 1994/2001, *In Search of Management*. Routledge.

A recent study focusing on the experience of middle managers in the wake of organizational restructuring is:

Hassard, John, McCann, Leo and Morris, Jonathan, 2009, *Managing in the Modern Corporation: The Intensification of Managerial Work in the USA, UK and Japan*. Cambridge University Press.

Also referred to in the text is:

Tengblad, Stefan, 2006, 'Is there a "New Managerial Work"? A comparison with Henry Mintzberg's classic study 30 years later', *Journal of Management Studies*, 43(7): 1437–62.

For an introduction to leadership see:

Grint, Keith, 2010, *Leadership: A Very Short Introduction*. Oxford University Press.

The studies of leadership referred to in the text, still worth reading despite their age, are:

Bennis, Warren, 1990, *Why Leaders Can't Lead: The Unconscious Conspiracy Continues*. Jossey Bass. Quotation from p. 18.

Kotter, John P., 1990, *A Force for Change: How Leadership Differs from Management*. Free Press. For highlights see Kotter, 1990, 'What leaders really do', *Harvard Business Review*, 68(3): 103–11.

Zaleznik, Abraham, 1977, 'Managers and Leaders: are they different?', *Harvard Business Review*, 55(3): 67–78, reprinted 2004 in 82(1): 74–81.

Chapter 3: Management and authority

Weber's accounts of authority and bureaucracy can be found in:

Weber, Max, 1947, *The Theory of Social and Economic Organization*. Edited with an introduction by Talcott Parsons. Free Press.

Weber, Max, 1978, *Economy and Society*. University of California Press.

Both are based on the original (1922) German publication, *Wirtschaft und Gesellschaft*, the 1947 translation being restricted to Part 1 of this work. The quotations are taken from the 1947 edition, pages 337 ('superior to any other form…') and 329 ('The idea that…'). An extract of the key passage is reprinted on pp. 3–15 of:

Pugh, Derek, ed., 2008, *Organization Theory: Selected Classical Readings*. 5th edition. Penguin.

Although Fayol's work is very widely cited, it is rarely read now, but there is a substantial extract in the Pugh volume just cited, pp. 253–74. The book itself is available as:

Fayol, Henri, 1984, *General and Industrial Management*. IEEE.

For a short history of management in terms of competing rational and normative tendencies see:

Barley, Stephen R. and Kunda, Gideon, 1991, 'Design and devotion: surges of rational and normative ideologies of control in managerial discourse', *Administrative Science Quarterly*, 37(3): 363–99.

For the early history of management see:

Bendix, Reinhard, 2001 (original edition 1956), *Work and Authority in Industry: Managerial Ideologies in the Course of Industrialization*. Transaction.

Chandler, Alfred D., Jr., 1977, *The Visible Hand: The Managerial Revolution in American Business*. Harvard University Press.

Nelson, Daniel, 1996, *Managers and Workers: Origins of the New Factory System in the United States, 1880–1920*. 2nd edition. University of Wisconsin Press.

Wren, Daniel A. and Bedeian, Arthur G., 2009, *The Evolution of Management Thought*. 6th edition. Wiley.

Other works referred to in the text are:

Faulks, Sebastian, 1993, *Birdsong*. Hutchinson.

Tönnies, Ferdinand, 2001 (original German edition 1887), *Community and Civil Society*. Cambridge University Press.

Chapter 4: Rationalizing management

The work of Fayol and some general histories are referenced under Chapter 3. The other key works referred to in this chapter are, in order of reference:

Taylor, Frederick W., 1911, *The Principles of Scientific Management*. Harper.

Drucker, Peter F., 1954, *The Practice of Management*. Harper & Row.

Many of Drucker's contributions are included in his 2011 volume, *The Essential Drucker*. Routledge. The quotation is from p. 90 of this volume.

Odiorne, George S., 1965, *Management by Objectives: A System of Managerial Leadership*. Pitman.

Packard, David, 2006, *The HP Way: How Bill Hewlett and I Built our Company*. Harper Business.

Ansoff, H. Igor, 1958, 'Strategies for diversification', *Harvard Business Review*, 36 (September–October): 113–24.

Ansoff, H. Igor, 1965/1988, *Corporate Strategy*. Penguin.

Porter, Michael E., 1980, *Competitive Strategy: Techniques for Analyzing Industries and Competitors*. Free Press.

Porter, Michael E., 1985, *Competitive Advantage: Creating and Sustaining Superior Performance*. Free Press.

Prahalad, C. K. and Hamel, Gary, 1990, 'The core competence of the corporation', *Harvard Business Review*, 68(3): 79–91.

Lindblom, Charles E., 1969, 'The science of muddling through', *Public Administration*, 19(1): 79–88. This is reprinted in full in Pugh, *Organization Theory* (see above under Chapter 4), 278–95.

Cohen, Michael D., March, James G. and Olsen, Johan P., 1972, 'A garbage can model of organizational choice', *Administrative Science Quarterly*, 17(1): 1–25, quote from p. 1. See also March, James G., 1988, *Decisions and Organizations*. Blackwell.

Janis, Irving L., 1972, *Victims of Groupthink*. Houghton Mifflin.

Janis, Irving L. 1989, *Crucial Decisions: Leadership in Policymaking and Crisis Management*. Free Press.

Kahneman Daniel, Slovic, Paul and Tversky, Amos, 1982, *Judgement under Uncertainty: Heuristics and Biases*. Cambridge University Press.

Kahneman, Daniel and Tversky, Amos, 1979, 'Prospect theory: An analysis of decisions under risk', *Econometrica*, 47 (2): 263–91.

Kahneman, Daniel, 2011, *Thinking, Fast and Slow*. Allen Lane.

Chandler, Alfred D., Jr., 1962, *Strategy and Structure*. MIT Press.

Burns, Tom and Stalker, G. M., 1961, *The Management of Innovation*. Tavistock Institute.

Lawrence, Paul R. and Lorsch, Jay W., 1967, *Organization and Environment*. Harvard University Press.

Vroom, Victor H., 1974, 'A new look at managerial decision making', *Organizational Dynamics*, 5(1): 66–80. Excerpted in Pugh, *Organization Theory* (see above under Chapter 4), 309–28.

Fiedler, Fred E., 1967, *A Theory of Leadership Effectiveness*. McGraw-Hill.

Mintzberg, Henry, 1983, *Structure in Fives: Designing Effective Organizations*. Prentice-Hall. Much of this material is also covered in his 1989 volume, *Mintzberg on Management*. Free Press.

Hammer, Michael, 1990, 'Reengineeering work: don't automate, obliterate', *Harvard Business Review*, 68(4): 104–12. A fuller account is in Hammer, Michael and Champy, James A., 1993, *Reengineering the Corporation: A Manifesto for Business Revolution*. Harper Business.

Davenport, Thomas, 1993, *Process Innovation: Reengineering Work Through Information Technology*. Harvard Business School Press.

The various strategic management models can be found in any business strategy textbook, the most rigorous and the most accessible being, respectively:

Grant, Robert M., 2009, *Competitive Strategy Analysis*. 7th edition.

Johnson, Gerry, Whittington, Richard and Scholes, Kevan, 2010, *Exploring Strategy*. FT Prentice Hall.

The most readable and thought-provoking account of decision making in the context of various theories then current remains:

Alisson, Graham T., 1971, *Essence of Decision: Explaining the Cuban Missile Crisis*. Longman.

The origins of SWOT analysis (Figure 2(a)) are unclear. It began appearing in textbooks in the 1970s, but with various attributions. The other visualizations in Figures 2–5 are based on the following accounts:

Figure 2(b): Ansoff, 'Strategies for diversification'.

Figure 2(c): Boston Consulting Group, 1970, 'The product portfolio' at www.bcg.com/documents/file13255.pdf.

Figure 3(a), (b): Porter, *Competitive Strategy*, chapters 1 and 2.

Figure 3(c): Porter, *Competitive Advantage*.

Figure 4: Prahalad and Hamel, 'The core competence of the corporation'.

Figure 5: Mintzberg, *Mintzberg on Management*, chapter 6.

Chapter 5: Socializing management

For the history of betterment and paternalism see:

Brandes, Stuart D., 1970, *American Welfare Capitalism: 1880–1940*. Chicago University Press.

Tone, Andrea, 1997, *The Business of Benevolence*. Cornell University Press.

An entertaining and thought-provoking exploration of some of the thinking associated with the expansion of these programmes in the 20th century can be found in a history of public relations:

Marchand, Roland, 2001, *Creating the Corporate Soul*. University of California Press.

For general histories of the management ideas discussed here, see the article by Barley and Kunda and the book by Wren and Bedeian cited for Chapter 3. The key works referred to in this chapter are, in order of reference:

McGregor, Douglas M., 1960, *The Human Side of Enterprise*. McGraw-Hill.

Mayo, Elton, 1933, *The Human Problems of an Industrial Civilization*. Macmillan.

Roethlisberger, Fritz J. and Dickson, William J., 1939, *Management and the Worker*. Harvard University Press.

Barnard, Chester, 1938, *The Functions of the Executive*. Harvard University Press.

Likert, Rensis, 1961, *New Patterns of Management*. McGraw-Hill.

Maslow, Abraham, 1954, *Motivation and Personality*. Harper.

Herzberg, Frederick, 1966, *Work and the Nature of Man*. World Publishing.

Trist, Eric L. et al., 1990–97, *The Social Engagement of Social Science: A Tavistock Anthology*. University of Pennsylvania Press.

Lewin, Kurt, 1951, *Field Theory in Social Science*. Harper and Row.

Rogers, Carl, 1961, *On Becoming a Person: A Therapist's View of Psychotherapy*. Houghton Mifflin.

Pascale, Richard T. and Athos, Anthony G., 1981, *The Art of Japanese Management: Applications for American Executives*. Simon and Schuster.

Ouchi, William G., 1981, *Theory Z: How American Business can Meet the Japanese Challenge*. Addison-Wesley.

Deal, Terrence E. and Kennedy, Allan A., 1982, *Corporate Cultures*. Addison-Wesley.

Peters, Thomas J. and Waterman, Robert H., 1982, *In Search of Excellence*. Harper and Row.

Kanter, Rosabeth Moss, 1983, *The Change Masters: Innovation and Entrepreneurship in the American Corporation*. Simon and Schuster.

Academic works on organizational culture include:

Schein, Edgar, 1985, *Organizational Culture and Leadership*. Jossey-Bass.

Barney, Jay B., 1986, 'Organizational culture: can it be a source of sustainable competitive advantage?', *Academy of Management Review*, 11(3): 656–65.

Pondy, Louis R., Frost, Peter J., Morgan, Gareth and Dandridge, Thomas C., 1983, *Organizational Symbolism*. JAI Press.

On the difficulties facing attempts at culture change see:

Hendry, John and Hope, Veronica, 1994, 'Cultural change and competitive performance', *European Management Journal*, 12(4): 401–6.

Johnson, Gerry, 1992, 'Managing strategic change: strategy, culture and action', *Long Range Planning*, 25(1): 28–36.

Pettigrew, Andrew M. and Whipp, Richard, 1991, *Managing Change for Competitive Success*. Blackwell.

For a critical perspective on the developments discussed in this chapter, see:

Boltanski, Luc and Chiapello, Eve, 2007, *The New Spirit of Capitalism*. Verso.

Chapter 6: Individualizing management

I have explored the themes of this chapter in much more detail in:

Hendry, John, 2004, *Between Enterprise and Ethics: Business and Management in a Bimoral Society*. Oxford University Press.

The two classic sociological studies referred to are:

Dalton, Melville, 1959, *Men Who Manage: Fusions of Feeling and Theory in Administration*. Wiley.

Jackall, Robert, 1988, *Moral Mazes: The World of Corporate Managers*. Oxford University Press.

A third such study, which captures the relationship between the traditional American corporation, its managers, and their families, is:

Kanter, Rosabeth Moss, 1977/1993, *Men and Women of the Corporation*. Basic Books.

Amongst the most insightful and at the same time accessible accounts of the social and psychological changes accompanying the rise of enterprise culture are:

Bellah, Robert N., et al., 1985/1996, *Habits of the Heart: Individualism and Commitment in American Life*. University of California Press.

Sennett, Richard, 1998, *The Corrosion of Character: The Personal Consequences of Work in the New Capitalism*. Norton.

The nearest thing to a manifesto for enterprise itself in a management context is:

Gilder, George, 1984/1986, *The Spirit Of Enterprise*. Simon and Schuster/Penguin.

On the audit culture and the failure of financial audit, see, respectively:

Power, Michael, 1999, *The Audit Society: Rituals of Verification*. Oxford University Press.

Hendry, John, 2013, *Ethics and Finance: An Introduction*. Cambridge University Press.

Chapter 7: Management across cultures

The key sources for this chapter are:

Hampden-Turner, Charles and Trompenaars, Alfons, 1993, *The Seven Cultures of Capitalism*. Doubleday.

Hampden-Turner, Charles and Trompenaars, Alfons, 1998, *Riding the Waves of Culture: Understanding Diversity in Global Business*. McGraw-Hill.

Hofstede, Geert, 1980/2001, *Culture's Consequences: International Differences in Work Related Values*. Sage.

Hofstede, Geert, 1991/2010, *Cultures and Organizations: Software of the Mind*. McGraw-Hill.

Table 1 is based on data reported in *The Seven Cultures of Capitalism* and Figure 6 is adapted from the figures on p. 77 of this work. These are very impressionistic and appear slightly differently in *Riding the Waves of Culture*. Table 2 is based on data obtainable at geert-hofstede.com, which gives values and analysis on five dimensions across 93 countries.

A particularly insightful comparison of French and American cultures can be found in:

Lamont, Michelle, 1992, *Cultures, Morals and Manners*. University of Chicago Press.

Chapter 8: Critical perspectives on management

For a textbook introduction to the approach of critical management studies, see:

Knights, David and Willmott, Hugh, 1999, *Management Lives. Power and identity in Work Organizations.* Sage.

For more advanced introductions, see:

Alvesson, Mats and Willmott, Hugh, 2012, *Making Sense of Management: A Critical Introduction.* 2nd edition. Sage.
Alvesson, Mats, Bridgman, Todd and Willmott, Hugh, eds, 2011, *The Oxford Handbook of Critical Management Studies.* Oxford University Press.

For the plight of junior managers, see the book by Hassard and others referred to in Chapter 2. Shorter works of particular interest for their insights to the emergence of business strategy and the American adaptation of Japanese management techniques respectively are:

Knights, David and Morgan, Glenn, 1991, 'Corporate strategy, organizations and subjectivity: a critique', *Organization Studies,* 12: 251–73.
Willmott, Hugh, 1993, 'Strength is ignorance, slavery is freedom: managing culture in modern organisations', *Journal of Management Studies,* 30(4): 515–52.

Other works referenced in this chapter, in order of mention, are:

Marx, Karl, 1887 (1867), *Capital.* Available online and in many editions.
Berle, Adolph A., Jr and Means, Gardiner, 1932, *The Modern Corporation and Private Property.* Commerce Clearing House.
Shleifer, Andrei and Vishny, Robert, 1997, 'A survey of corporate governance', *Journal of Finance,* 52: 737–83, quote on p. 738.
McIntyre, Alasdair, 1985, *After Virtue: A Study in Moral Theory.* 2nd edition. Duckworth. Quote on p. 74.
Deetz, Stanley A., 1992, *Democracy in an Age of Corporate Colonization: Developments in Communication and the Politics of Everyday Life.* SUNY Press.

Chapter 9: Management as sense-making

The classic account of sense-making, and an excellent guide to other writings, is:

Weick, Karl, 1995, *Sensemaking in Organizations*. Sage.

Other important works referred to are:

Garfinkel, Harold, 1967, *Studies in Ethnomethodology*. Prentice Hall.

Milgram, Stanley, 1963, 'Behavioral study of obedience', *Journal of Abnormal and Social Psychology*, 67: 371–8.

The Milgram experiments have also been the subject of a number of television documentaries, some of which can be found on YouTube.

A good textbook introduction to the management of change is:

Balogun, Julia, Hailey, Veronica Hope, Johnson, Gerry and Scholes, Kevan, 2003, *Exploring Strategic Change*. FT Prentice Hall.

Two works of fiction that nicely illustrate some of the ideas in this chapter, the first implicitly, the second more explicitly, are:

Tolstoy, Leo, 1869/2010, *War and Peace*. Oxford University Press. Also in many other translations and editions.

Barnes, Julian, 2006, *Arthur and George*. Vintage.

Chapter 10: Management and morality

For a much fuller treatment of these issues, see Hendry, *Between Enterprise and Ethics*, cited under Chapter 6.

Also referred to in this chapter is:

Bauman, Zygmunt, 1989, *Modernity and the Holocaust*. Polity.

Index

J

K

L

M

ONLINE CATALOGUE
A Very Short Introduction

Our online catalogue is designed to make it easy to find your ideal Very Short Introduction. View the entire collection by subject area, watch author videos, read sample chapters, and download reading guides.

http://fds.oup.com/www.oup.co.uk/general/vsi/index.html

SOCIAL MEDIA
Very Short Introduction

Join our community

www.oup.com/vsi

- Join us online at the official Very Short Introductions **Facebook** page.
- Access the thoughts and musings of our authors with our online **blog**.
- Sign up for our monthly **e-newsletter** to receive information on all new titles publishing that month.
- Browse the full range of Very Short Introductions online.
- Read **extracts** from the Introductions for free.
- Visit our library of **Reading Guides**. These guides, written by our expert authors' will help you to question again, why you think what you think.
- If you are a teacher or lecturer you can order inspection copies quickly and simply via our website.